FROM THE PULPIT
TO THE BEDSIDE

FROM THE PULPIT TO THE BEDSIDE

Sermons from a Physician-Pastor

Benjamin Rolin Doolittle

ISBN: 1523205490
ISBN 13: 9781523205493

To the Hand in My Hand
To The Mermaids

Table of Contents

Welcome

I am a physician and a pastor. While I love medicine and the ministry, I confess to my ambivalence about both. Churches can be exasperating places, disappointing and deflating given that the stakes are so high. Equally so the hospital, where burnout is rampant and cover-your-ass protocols so often replace thoughtful medicine. In medicine, it is so easy for the computer, the labs, all of it to get in the way of the patient's real needs. I confess that I am, at times, as crotchety as any of the most jaded pastor or physician. And yet, when the church is "on," there is no sweeter place. The hospital is one of the best places to behold wondrous healing and daily miracles, were our eyes open more often.

I teach on the faculty of a medical school where I serve in the clinics and the wards. I am board certified in internal medicine and pediatrics. On weekends, I slam out shifts in a community hospital emergency room. I have also been a pastor for more than 25 years. My joy has been to serve the urban church – usually with congregations who cannot afford a full time (or even part time) pastor.

As the years go by, I have evolved a desperate faith, childlike almost, aching and visceral. As a medical school professor, I am steeped in a grand intellectual tradition. I am also a pastor who has found joy and meaning in my Christian faith. Because of these two roles, I feel a gut-level, desperate need that faith must be real and relevant. There is too much suffering, too much worry, too much grief for faith to be an abstraction or an intellectual exercise. These sermons are my attempt to keep faith real to me and relevant to my world.

To compile these sermons assumes a certain amount of hubris: who would bother to read these words? Much of my life's work in the ministry and in medicine has been one of translation – forging the gap between the world of soul and mind. With my patients, I broach spiritual issues all the time. As medical school faculty, I often have the honor to don my preaching robes and officiate in many wonderful weddings. In the church, I explain medical issues and help folks navigate the complicated world of the hospital. Medicine, I find, is often safe introductory territory towards deeper conversation.

This is a compilation of sermons preached throughout the past 17 years: most as sermons from various churches and a few presentations from various medical conferences. I have cleaned them up a bit for flow and clarity, but not so much to lose the sermon feel. These chapters are meditations, stories, and parables, words delivered with love in hopes of sharing good news. They are loosely arranged to connect how one might discover the faith – Living, Suffering, Thinking, Hoping, Loving. We live. We suffer as everyone does. We reflect upon our suffering. We hope, yearn, and ache for an answer. We discover God's love, a gift. I hope these words are accessible to the doubter as well as to the believer. In the end, this collection is a humble offering of my own journey, that it may give insight into your own.

Onwards in hope,
Ben

Introduction

Doctors, the real ministers of our age (?)

Does religion make a difference? Does church? Faith? If you attend church regularly, do you live long? How many more years do you live? Three? Seven? Fourteen? Negative 7 (because we spend too much time eating cake at coffee hour)?

The answer is 7 if you are Caucasian and 14 if you are African American.[*]

Another study looked at suicidality. Did you know what the strongest risk factor for suicidality was? Lack of attendance at church. People who never attended church were 4 times as likely to commit suicide.[†] This is a stronger effect than alcohol or drugs. Part of the reason for this, of course, is that people using alcohol and drugs are in our congregations.

In the same kind of study, cities with the highest church attendance had the lowest suicide rate. For every 1% decline in attendance, 1.4% increase in suicide.[‡]

One study looked at children with cystic fibrosis. What percentage of patients used "religious treatments" (prayer, pilgrimages, talismans – that sort of thing)? 20%? 40%? 60%?[§] The answer, of course, is 60%. This is incredibly important. Cystic fibrosis is very complicated to treat and re-

[*] Hummer, Robert A., Richard G. Rogers, Charles B. Nam, and Christopher G. Ellison. "Religious involvement and US adult mortality." *Demography* 36, no. 2 (1999): 273-285.

[†] Comstock, George W., and Kay B. Partridge. "Church attendance and health." *Journal of chronic diseases* 25, no. 12 (1972): 665-672.

[‡] Stack, Steven. "The effect of the decline in institutionalized religion on suicide, 1954-1978." *Journal for the Scientific Study of Religion* (1983): 239-252.

[§] Stern, Robert C., Edward R. Canda, and Carl F. Doershuk. "Use of nonmedical treatment by cystic fibrosis patients." *Journal of Adolescent Health* 13, no. 7 (1992): 612-615.

quires a complicated multi-disciplinary approach to care. It's really, really important that doctors know that their patients are seeking religious oriented treatments.

Did you know that if a chaplain visits a patient recuperating from a hip fracture, the patient gives higher satisfaction scores, uses less pain medication, and gets discharged from the hospital sooner? Amazing, right. Imagine if there were a procedure or a drug that could do all that. Well, we all know there is: you.

I share all this because I find it so interesting and so important. All of those studies confirm what we already know: our spiritual lives are important. A matter of life or death, or at least health and wellness.

I consider myself fully in. I am full on physician – with all the baggage that comes with that. I am trained in that evidence based tradition. I work the data. I am Dr. Doolittle after all. Believe me, there is a lot of baggage with that name.

I am also a full on pastor – and have been so for more than 20 years. Being a pastor isn't easy. I was a solo pastor of small churches in New Haven for 14 years – all through medical school, residency, and my early years on the faculty. Only after I started having kids did I jump in as an associate pastor, which I am today.

"DOCTORS ARE THE MINISTERS FOR THIS AGE."
I would like to use our time to wrestle with an incident that happened….

When I was a medical student, I was the pastor of a small congregation in New Haven – Pilgrim Congregational Church. It was a great place. Beautiful people. They didn't have a lot of money to afford a full time guy (or even a part time guy) and so they were stuck with me, a divinity school who later went on to medical school.

I would write my sermons on hospital notepaper while I was on call in the hospital. I would sit in the nurse's station and poke through the scripture, jot thoughts down, and stay close with the patients.

My attending physician – my supervisor – approached me and asked what I was doing. I told him. He said, "Doolittle, don't you know that doctors are the real ministers for this age?"

I have thought a lot about that statement. Initially, I thought he was teasing me, or chiding, or baiting me into a debate. Maybe he was areligious or anti-religious. Hard to say. But over the years, I've thought a lot about that statement. "Doctors are the ministers for this age." "Doctors are the ministers for this age."

I have come to the conclusion that he is absolutely right and absolutely wrong, at exactly the same time.

There is a hierarchy to medicine that looks very similar to the hierarchy of the church. Both professions wear liturgical garb. Through both disciplines, there is a distinct language and tradition that you are adopted into. From 30,000 feet, the two professions look a lot alike.

Patients come to their doctors with heavy hearts. They want to feel better. They come for reassurance that they are not going to die. They come to unburden themselves. They come to confess. How do I know this? Because some of my interactions with my patients look a lot like my interactions with my parishioners. People are hurting and seek all sorts of ways to get better.

At the same time, doctors do not offer what ministers offer. We doctors love to hide behind our medicine. Medical problems are always safe problems. We use a coded language. There is always another test to order, always another specialist to refer to. We doctors love to turn spiritual problems into medical problems.

And so, all to often, I think the patient is left dissatisfied. Why do I still have headaches? Why do I still have abdominal pains? Why am I so nervous all the time?

The very notion that a physician can occupy the space of a minister is horribly wrong. Maybe one thing we physicians can do is actively engage with our patients' spiritual lives. It's not really that hard. In medical school, we are trained to ask what kind of drugs you use, who you have sex with, how much you drink. You would think that it wouldn't be hard for us to say, "I've heard that religion helps people live healthier lives, have you thought about reconnecting with church, with your synagogue, with a religious community." More and more medical schools are training students about the importance of religion.

"Physicians are the ministers for this age." Yes and no. For reasons that are both right and tragically wrong. But if we physicians could be more like ministers lots of beautiful things could happen.

THE STORY OF ROSA...
I learned this lesson the hard way. I met Rosa on the day she was diagnosed with HIV. She had not been feeling well and went to the public health department. The test came back positive. And so, they put her in my schedule. I was a resident at the time.

When I met her, she was sitting in the chair, doubled over, clutching her sides, rocking back and forth, and saying over and over, "I am going to die. I am going to die. I know that I am going to die."

Turns out, her viral load – the amount of HIV in her body was 500,000. That's a lot of HIV. Her T cell count, a marker of her immune system was 10. A normal t-cell count is around 500. And so, by any account, she was right. There was a good chance that she was going to die.

There were wonderful social workers and other people got involved. HIV medicine is pretty easy actually. If you take your medicine properly, the HIV viral load becomes undetectable, and the t-cell count bounces back – restoring somewhat the immune system. I simply this, of course, because where HIV becomes complicated is managing all the chronic long-term side effects.

Anyway, Rosa takes her medications. And that is precisely what happens. Dramatically so. Her viral load plunges to become undetectable. Her t cell count creeps back into the normal range – which is pretty amazing given how low it was when she started.

I was seeing her just about every month. I learned that she started going to church and became very heavily involved. A few committees and then she started teaching Sunday School. She would speak warmly of her church, how supportive it was, how her life had blossomed.

On one of our visits, her viral load was again undetectable. Her t-cell count was again close to the normal range.

"Congratulations," I say with that air of self-satisfaction. "Your blood work is great. You are doing so well taking all of your medications."

Rosa looks at me with this mischievous twinkle in her eye and a wry grin. "Doctor, I need to tell you something. I stopped taking my medications."
    "When did you stop?" I ask.
    "Six months ago," she says.
    "Why?" I ask, more than a bit flummoxed.
    "Because I believe that God has healed me of my HIV."

What do you say next? She didn't need a doctor. She needed a pastor. She didn't need a pill. She needed theology. We talked a long time. She was absolutely against taking medications. She knew, for sure, that God had healed her. I didn't want to create this conflict between her faith and her medical care. And so, we called in the social worker. We said a prayer in the clinic office. We decided that she would come in and see me every 3 months. We would check labs. We would continue the conversation. We would pray together. If I felt she was reaching a point of danger with her blood counts, we would discuss the issue of medications again.

Turns out, she was cured – almost. Her viral load remained undetectable for more than 2 years - practically a miracle. Her t-cell count remained within the normal range for many, many years. We continued the conversation. Her viral load began to creep up. Her t-cells began to drop. Then, it was time. She needed to take her medications. At that time, she was ready. Her medications were a gift from God. She needed to stay healthy so she could serve in the church. She had a mission for her life. Medications squared with her mission. And so it goes. We have been together for a long time now. On medications, her viral load is undetectable. Her t-cell count is within the normal range.

What did Rosa really need? A physician to prescribe a pill? That was the easy part. What she needed was a pastor.

"Physicians are the ministers for this age." Yes and no.

One of the most important lessons I learned about church was when I was between churches, wondering what the next step was in my ministry. That first Sunday that I had off, I slept late, made a cup of coffee, and sipped it on the back patio. It was a glorious summer day, earlier enough to be warm, but not too hot. Birds at the feeder. Tomatoes getting plump on the fine. The cat asleep in the chair next to me.

And that is when I realized something really important. Going to church is really important. My faith, my relationship with Jesus Christ, my commitment to the church is at the core of my being. But at that moment, that cup of coffee was more important than church. I realize that maybe what I said was blasphemous for a company man, but I suspect, I believe, that is exactly what goes through the mind and hearts of many of our parishioners.

Is my church life more important than that cup of coffee? Is that cup of coffee more relevant at that moment than my church experience?

I know that if I make it to church, I will love it. But the clock is ticking and I need to get up from my chair in 5 minutes or else I will be late. And if I'm late, that's so embarrassing, I might as well have a second cup of coffee.

That is our challenge. Church is life or death: spiritually as well as physically. I don't know if our people really feel that in the same immediate way. Have we seceded our relevance to the doctors or the politicians?

I offered a few thoughts about that line, "Physicians are the ministers for the age." That is not exactly true. The prophet Jeremiah had something to say about physicians of his age, "Since my people are crushed, I am crushed; I mourn, and horror grips me. Is there no balm in Gilead? Is there no physician there? When then is there no healing for the wound of my people? (Jeremiah 8:21-22) Jesus had something to say about physicians, "It is not the healthy who need a doctor, but the sick." (Mark 2:17)

I wonder what happens when we flip the saying, "Ministers are the physicians for the age." I have a story about all this idea of relevance and our shared purpose to bring good news to the world....

I RING THE BELL
My first position in the ministry was at Pilgrim Congregational Church. I was a first year divinity school student. One of the deans sent me over to Pilgrim because they were between ministers. They had financial

problems and they were contemplating closing. "Just go over there and preach while they figure out what they are going to do…."

I borrow a preaching robe, drink a gallon of coffee, and pull an all-nighter to craft the sermon. The next morning, I grab hold of the pulpit as hard as I can and just let it go. They ask me to preach the next Sunday, and then the Sunday after that.

Around the fourth or fifth Sunday, I notice a rope hanging in the narthex. I know what this rope is. This is the rope that, as a kid, under penalty of eternal damnation, I was never allowed to touch. This is the rope that connects to the bell high up in the steeple. By this time, I had preached four, maybe five sermons. Surely I, as clergy, would have license to ring the bell.

Enter two church guys. The first is Oscar Bamford, the head lay leader of the church, and Eisten Nordstrum, the other head lay leader of the church. They are both in their 70's and they have loved this church for most of their lives. In time, I come to call Oscar affectionately the "Big O", and Eisten, "Ace." From the beginning, they called me "kid," because I was one.
　　"Big O, I want to pull that rope," I say.
　　"Knock yourself out, Kid," says the Big O.
　　I grab the rope. I heave my weight against the rope. The rope does not budge. The bell does not ring.
　　"We haven't heard it ring in years," says Ace.
　　"We just stopped ringing the bell," says the Big O. "I dunno, we just forgot about the durn thing."

Someone gets an idea – maybe Ace, maybe the Big O. I am sure it was not mine. We meet on a Saturday morning to investigate. We open the door trap door into the steeple and climb the dusty, rickety stairs. The dark cave smells like a sauna. From cracks in the wall, beams of light catch the dust. At the top of the stairs, there is a steep ladder. Ace looks at the Big O, who then looks at me, "Go ahead kid, this was your idea."

We climb the steep ladder. I am certain that we are the first human beings to stand on the rungs of this ladder in the last 20? 50? 100 years? Since the civil war? At the top of the steep ladder, there is another ladder. This final ladder is made out of cobwebs and termite spit.

Ace and the Big O look at me. They do not speak. I do not want to wimp out. I do not want to be some geeky, awkward, wimpy seminary guy – even though that was exactly what I was, and everyone knew it.

Ace looks at me and smiles, "I'll go first." He takes to the rungs. Big O is, well, big. "You'd better go."

We are in the belly of this old New England church steeple. We are impossibly high. Breathtakingly high. If this ladder goes, there will be some serious damage to all sorts of body parts.

There is a trap door. We push against the trap door. The door does not budge. We lean our shoulders into the trap door. The door does not budge. We heave into the trap door. Nothing.

I have a brilliant idea. I go to my car – a 1986 Chevie Citation. I get the car jack. I climb the stairs. I climb the ladder. I climb up through the cobwebs. I jam the car jack between the top rung of the cobweb ladder and the trap door. I crank the car jack.

There is a loud crack. Something breaks. We are not falling. It is the trap door. But we cannot see. I crank the car jack. Crack. The trap door opens.

No *human* had been up there for 100 years. For the past 100 years, however, the church steeple was the luxury condominium complex for many, many generations of pigeons.

I turn the crank one more time. At that moment, a tidal wave of genera-tions' worth of pigeon guano crashes right into our faces. There is a sting to our eyes, a very unnerving crunch in our teeth, and a sick, sandpaper feeling dribbling down our skin. The pigeons are very pissed off.

But I knew that I had come to the right place. When the good Lord casts down 100 years worth of pigeon shit right on your head, you know you are in the right place. I get the message. I am hooked. I love this place.

Fast forward a few weeks, after a work crew cleaned out the steeple. It is Sunday morning. Big O and Ace look at me, "Go ahead, this was your idea." I was sure it was not my idea, but I am honored to comply. I pull the rope with all my might. The heave of the bell sweeps me off my feet. 100 feet up, a bell chimes in the spring air. I fly up to the sky, holding onto the rope for dear life. And it is very good, very good indeed.

This is our job. This is what we are to do with our lives: ring the bell. To ring the bell means we must first clean out the pigeon schtuff from the steeple.

What I mean is this: we must do what needs to be done if it supports our mission. Our mission is to bring good news, articulate a vision for our world that offers something besides reality TV shows, be a presence of hope in a world that seems always to be hurting.

Slogging pigeon guano was not in the job description, but it became the symbol of everything I did at Pilgrim Church. I was not perfect. But the church's bell still rings. I left after graduation from medical school to go overseas for a year.

"Ministers are the physicians for the age." It's a matter of life and death – that's what the data say. That's what the Bible says. We can offer our people good news, a safe port in a stormy world, a clear bell-song amidst the noise,

This is number 1 in our job description – to be the healers of this world: I ring the bell. I do what needs to be done to support the mission – to be healers of this world. I ring the bell. I ring the bell. I ring the bell.

Living

The Backpack and the Big Barn

Someone in the crowd said to him, "Teacher, tell my brother to divide the family inheritance with me." But he said to him, "Friend, who set me to be a judge or arbitrator over you?" And he said to them, "Take care! Be on your guard against all kinds of greed; for one's life does not consist in the abundance of possessions." Then he told them a parable: "The land of a rich man produced abundantly. And he thought to himself, 'What should I do, for I have no place to store my crops?' Then he said, 'I will do this: I will pull down my barns and build larger ones, and there I will store all my grain and my goods. And I will say to my soul, Soul, you have ample goods laid up for many years; relax, eat, drink, be merry.' But God said to him, 'You fool! This very night your life is being demanded of you. And the things you have prepared, whose will they be?' So it is with those who store up treasures for themselves but are not rich toward God."

~ LUKE 12:13-21

I graduated medical school in 1997. I was the only person in my class that did not go off to do a residency training program right away. Instead, I spent a year as a medical missionary. I went to India for six months and then to Honduras for six months where I served as a doctor to small, rural, church-affiliated hospitals.

When I left, I put all of my worldly possession into a backpack. Everything I needed for an entire year went into a backpack – and that included a huge medical textbook. Towards the end of my time in India, I scaled down even more. For the last 3 weeks, I traveled across India and I put all of my possessions in to a book-bag. By then, it wasn't a big deal really: I didn't have that much stuff anymore. I didn't want to schlep any more than I had to across India. Simplify. Simplify. Simplify.

Fast forward 14 years. Christine, my wife, and I have bought our first home. We want to renovate. The kitchen is 50 years old. We've accumulated a ton of stuff. Where am I going to keep my backpack? We hire an architect and a builder. We are going to blow out walls, dig deep holes, everything.

Our builder asks me, "Ben, I can build you a small barn, a medium sized barn, or a big barn. What would you like?" I think about all the priceless treasures that have filled my basement over the past 14 years – the pile of books from seminary, an old computer that I can't bear to throw away, the second hand desk that I've been meaning to paint, the Christmas tree ornaments, the Christmas tree. Without blinking an eye, I say, "A Big Barn."

When I read the passage this Sunday, I feel a lump in my throat. Like no other passage, I approach this spiritual lesson with humility, fear, and trembling. Can I possibly be redeemed? Am I the most superficial minister ever? Just what is going on in this passage?

In the book of Luke, Jesus talks a lot about money. Luke 18, he tells a rich man, "You still lack one thing. Sell all your possession and follow me." In Luke 19 is the story of Zacchaeus the tax collector who gives half of his possessions to the poor. In Luke 11, Jesus rebukes the Pharisees, "You give a tenth of your possessions, but you neglect justice and love of God." In Luke 10 is the story of the Good Samaritan.

And so, here is one more story about money. A man asks Jesus, "Tell my brother to divide the family inheritance with me." (Luke 12:13)

Back in the day, there were no civil courts per se. It fell to the Rabbis to arbitrate these sorts of legal disputes using Biblical law, fairness, precedent, etc. But Jesus is not a card-carrying Rabbi. He is the son of a carpenter from Nazareth.

Why does the man ask Jesus about his brother? My guess is that the man expected a supportive answer in his favor. It's the same thing when you are listening to a sermon and you think, "Oh yeah, my brother needs to hear this sermon. It would straighten him right out." Jesus is all about justice, fairness, and upsetting the old ways. It would be expected that Jesus would say, "Follow the law," where the eldest would receive a double portion, or perhaps he would say, "Share and share alike." Either way, I would expect Jesus would advocate for fairness and justice.

Instead he tells this parable to teach us all a lesson. A rich man has so much wealth he wants to tear down his old barns and build bigger barns. But God says to him, "You fool. This very night, you life is being demanded of you. And those things you've accumulated, whose will they be?"

And then Jesus turns towards the crowd and says, "So it is with those who store up treasures for themselves but are not rich toward God."

Jesus talks a lot about money, but what is interesting is that nowhere does Jesus say, "I want your money." Jesus asks for many other things, but he does not ask for your money.

I believe we live in a society where we find it easier to talk about sex rather than money. We live in a society where sexual indiscretion is forgivable. Anthony Weiner can text photos of himself to strangers and still run for mayor with a straight face – and almost be a viable candidate. Who cares? Eliot Spitzer can have extramarital affairs with prostitutes and then run for elected office in New York. Amazing.

But then there is money. Same issue of the New York Times. Insider traders are going to jail. In the past 2 months, senior executives at several major financial institutions – KPMG, SAC, Black Rock Hedge Fund – are all going to jail for insider trading. If you break the public trust about money, you go to jail. Amazing. If you send lewd photographs over the Internet, you run for office. The world seems to say, "Have sex with whomever you want and I'll still vote for you, but don't mess with my money."

And I dare say, we in the church also have a hard time talking about money. Ministers get queasy when asking church folk for money. Church folks get queasy when the minister asks for money. Many will share stories about how other churches mishandled money or laid heavy guilt trips on people.

Jesus never says, "I want your money." Instead, I think Jesus treats money as a thermometer, or maybe a barometer, that measures the pressure of a person's faith, or maybe a mirror that reflects our understanding of God. This sounds really heavy, but this is what I mean. Paul says, "Faith, hope, and love abide. These three. But the greatest of these is love." If you do not have the smallest bit of love, you will be immune to the needs of others. You will judge them. You will see them as unworthy of your gifts. You will not give. I think many times people do not give simply because they are afraid, afraid of not having enough, afraid of falling father behind. We lack a faith that all will be well. We lack the hope that things will get better. We lack a theology of abundance – that whatever we have, we have enough.

I think Jesus challenges us to use money as a lens towards our own understanding of God. Do we give out of a sense of guilt or obligation? Does your giving flow from a generous heart? Is it tinged with guilt or regret? Is our money like a security blanket for a 3 year old?

There is a passage in the book of Exodus 33-34 where God tells Moses, "I will help you, but I will not be real to you. You will not see my glory." Moses said, "We want to see you glory. We want you to be real to us." God says, "Then strip off your ornaments."

In order for God to be real to the people of Israel, they needed to strip off their ornaments. For God to be real, they needed to be empty. They needed to empty their barns - with trust and without fear – to be filled by God. They needed to let go of their reality – their money – so that God's reality could fill their lives.

There is the line in Paul's letter to the Corinthians, "We preach Christ crucified: a stumbling block to Jews and foolishness to Gentiles, but to those whom God has called, but Jews and Greeks, Christ the power of God and the wisdom of God. For the foolishness of God is wiser than human wisdom and the weakness of God is stronger than human strength." (I Cor 1:23-25)

Jesus emptied his reality, became weak, died an unjust death, and yet overcame the hatred and violence of the world with power and love. That love changes my life because I realize that there is a reality beyond the stuff in my barn. That power changes my life, because that is where my true power lies – not in the stuff crowding my basement.

This is how you know that you are truly rich: when giving is a natural extension of your love and there is neither guilt nor remorse. This is how you can know that you are truly rich: when we are changed by God, when we can let it all go because we have lives filled with the abundance of God. And that is where our true wealth lies. Amen.

The Lepers on the Mount

"Blessed are you who are poor, for yours is the kingdom of God.
Blessed are you who are hungry now, for you will be filled.
Blessed are you who weep now, for you will laugh.
Blessed are you when people hate you, and when they ex-
clude you, revile you, and defame you on account of the
Son of Man. Rejoice in that day and leap for joy, for surely
your reward is great in heaven; for that is what their ances-
tors did to the prophets.
But woe to you who are rich, for you have received your
consolation.
Woe to you who are full now, for you will be hungry.
Woe to you who are laughing now, for you will mourn and
weep.
Woe to you when all speak well of you, for that is what their
ancestors did to the false prophets."

~ LUKE 6:20-26

Loving, Wonderful God, we bring to you our tears, our hunger, our hope. May the words of Your Gospel work in us that our tears might become smiles, our hunger satiated, our hope fulfilled. Bless these words that they might bring your glory. In Christ's name we pray, Amen.

I felt shame, but it was a double shame. This is a sermon about shame and hope. But the shame is a double shame. The time is August 1997. The place is Tamil Nadu, south India, high in the dusty hills, the back villages.

The truck we ride is loaded with medicine and bandages. From the hospital, we have driven a few hours to treat a very special group of people.

Crouched in the dust on the side of the road, a group of mostly men, some women. Hidden beneath a gray sari, a dirty bandage. The truck stops. The people rise to their feet. The appointed day, the appointed hour has come.

Leprosy. The people have leprosy. The workers Prakash and Ishmael have treated leprosy patients for a collective 20 years.

Hands turned to snubs of bone and flesh. Open sores. The flies. Why are there so many flies? A goat chews on some garbage. We open our tables, set up our trays of pills and bandages. Why are there so many flies? What is that smell?

Leprosy is caused by a bacteria that kills the nerves. You can neither feel your hands, nor your feet, nor your face. The tiniest cuts get infected. The infection spreads. Gangrene. The tissue is destroyed. The limbs get worn down. The cartilage of the face, for reasons that are still not clear, lose their consistency, so the eyebrows fall off, and the nose appears to melt into the face.

This is the shame that I feel, but it is a double shame. I witness the shame of the leprosy patients. The leprosy patients - the lepers - wear the shame of their disease as if it were a curse or a crime. They are ashamed of themselves, how they look, how they smell. You feel the shame like the heat from a fire. The weight of their shame that bends them over double, that casts their eyes to the ground. The shame wraps around them like a rag, hides them from the world.

The second part of the shame is my own shame. I feel ashamed in myself. I want to run. I want to get away. My brain knows the infection has burned itself out years ago, but when I hold their hand in my hand and dress their wounds, my heart cries out, "Could you catch this too? Could you become a leper too?" Then, I feel ashamed at myself, my own weakness of character, my lack of compassion, my petty selfishness.

When I was thinking about the scripture, I thought about India. I thought of this scene because I imagined the lepers, the sick, the ill coming to hear Christ for his first sermon – the sermon where he climbed a hill and preached hope and love and truth - his Sermon on the Mount. They would come from the hills, their hiding places. The weight of their shame bends their backs. I would witness their shame in their bent over backs, and then feel the heartburn of my own shame. I did not want to reach out. I was afraid and wanted to flee.

But this time, on this dusty hill in Israel, two thousand years ago, Jesus speaks.
"Blessed are you who are poor, for yours is the Kingdom of God."
"Promises, promises," the lepers say. "Show me. Show me."
"Blessed are you who are hungry now, for you will be filled."
"We have heard all this before. Empty words from a crazy prophet."
"Blessed are you who weep now, for you shall laugh."
"I weep so much, my well of tears has gone dry."
"Blessed are you when people hate you, exclude you, revile you on account of the Son of Man . . . for surely your reward is great in heaven."
"People hate me so much, I have fled to the hills. People revile me so, I cover my head in rags. I cannot even imagine a heaven."

But the lepers are curious by what this man Jesus says and they stay to hear him out. Then Jesus reaches out his hands. He holds the lepers' hands in his own and out grow new fingers, new toes. Their faces grow new smiles. They stand up straight, made anew by the touch of Christ.

Those lepers who were there knew the tears and hunger and agony of hell in their lifetimes. And they also experienced the pure rapture, the pure love of God. Their hands that had no feeling were healed and felt touch of Christ. Hell and heaven in their lifetimes. The bitter and the sweet.

Jesus' words were not empty promises, but words that had flesh. Paul writes, "Now if Christ is proclaimed as raised from the dead, how can some of you say there is no resurrection of the dead? If there is no resurrection of the dead, then Christ has not been raised; and if Christ has not been raised; and if Christ has not been raised, then our proclamation has been in vain and your faith has been in vain. If Christ has not been raised, your faith is futile and you are still in your sins." (I Corinthians 15:12-17)

When Paul writes these words, he was not writing to the lepers. They felt Christ's healing. They knew Christ rose from the dead just as surely as they could wrap their new fingers around a cup of soup. Those lepers did not all thank Jesus, as we know from other stories, but my hunch is that they knew Christ was special. Paul writes these words for you and me, modern sophisticated hip folks of the third millennium.

When we talk about Jesus Christ, we like to say many comfortable things about him. "Jesus,. what a nice guy." "Jesus, he was a really, really good teacher." Sometimes, we like to say mystical things that are not meant to offend. "Jesus, the Son of God, Word made flesh." Abstract. Poetic. Comfortable.

Jesus Christ is not comfortable. Jesus gives comfort, but he is not comfortable. Jesus Christ rose from the dead. We nailed him to a cross with real nails. We tortured him. We threw him in a cave. And just about when all hope was lost, he rose again - resurrection! This is not a comfortable story.

Paul points that if we do not believe that he rose from the dead, then the faith is all a bunch of empty promises. Christianity becomes a bushel basket of empty rules. If Christ did not rise from the dead, then Christianity is a collection of empty caverns, framed with stained glass windows.

I ask you this: What are you ashamed of? What weighs you down so much that it breaks your back? What is your shame that chases you to the hills, away from God, away from people, away from yourself? Are you ashamed of your past? Are you ashamed of your doubts? Are you ashamed of your fear? Are you ashamed of what you really think?

You do not have leprosy, but sometimes, you might feel that you do. We all have been ashamed. When the word became flesh, which is exactly what happened. Christ's words, his touch, gave flesh to those lepers that needed flesh.

The lepers found Jesus not because they believed in him necessarily, but that they wanted to be healed. Belief came later. That gives me comfort. I come to Jesus with my shame, not because I am good or that my belief is perfect, but only because I want to be healed. I want to be healed. I want my shame to be lifted from me. I want to stand up straight.
"Blessed are you who are poor, for yours is the Kingdom of God."
"Blessed are you who are hungry now, for you will be filled."
"Blessed are you who weep now, for you shall laugh."

The Christ who reaches out to them, reaches out to you. The Christ that heals them, heals you as well. The Christ who died for them, dies for you. Not because they were good, but because Christ loved them - the same way that Christ loves you. This is the Good News and the promise of the Gospel. Amen.

The Honkey Tonk & The Bucket List

Then he said to them, "These are my words that I spoke to you while I was still with you—that everything written about me in the law of Moses, the prophets, and the psalms must be fulfilled." Then he opened their minds to understand the scriptures, and he said to them, "Thus it is written, that the Messiah is to suffer and to rise from the dead on the third day, and that repentance and forgiveness of sins is to be proclaimed in his name to all nations, beginning from Jerusalem. You are witnesses of these things. And see, I am sending upon you what my Father promised; so stay here in the city until you have been clothed with power from on high." Then he led them out as far as Bethany, and, lifting up his hands, he blessed them. While he was blessing them, he withdrew from them and was carried up into heaven. And they worshiped him, and returned to Jerusalem with great joy; and they were continually in the temple blessing God.

~ LUKE 24:44-53

Loving God, we join the disciples in the temple, worshiping you. Open our minds to understanding and our hearts to your care. In Christ's name we pray, Amen.

A few weeks ago, I was in Nashville Tennessee, the capital of country music. I was there for a "very important" medical conference. As anyone who has ever been to a conference or convention will tell you, there is the *meeting* and then there is the *after-meeting.* There is the meeting where you might sit on a deliberative committee one session, then go hear a presentation at another session. Then, there is the after-meeting, where you catch up with old friends, get the latest news, great stuff.

To have the meeting in Nashville is good. But to have the after-meeting in Nashville, the capital of country western music, is great. The city is filled with juke joints, honkey tonks, bars, and saloons where every night of the week there is live music playing. They even pipe in country music at the cross walks. It's a friendly city where you can't help but have a tune on ·your lips and a bounce in your step.

As fate would have it, during the after-meeting, I found myself in a Nashville Honkey-tonk. Instead of a live band, it was karaoke night. In a city where everyone is trying to break into the country music scene, karaoke night is a big deal. There were some amazing singers. And then, all of sudden, my good friend Lenny from Baltimore, he was up there. He sang, "I got friends in low places." I could have been offended by this, but he did a great job. And then, Mike from Buffalo did a pretty good Willie Nelson cover, "On the road again." Someone from our conference I didn't know did a great Taylor Swift, "I knew you were trouble."

Standing in a Nashville Honkey-Tonk, on karaoke night, I realized that this is a bucket list moment. You know "The Bucket List." It's the list of things you want to do before you kick the bucket. If I didn't get up there to sing a song, I would regret this the rest of my life. But what song to sing? You think you know a lot of songs, but you realize that you don't know the whole song.

Because I am a Christian gentleman, I sang about one of our country's more enduring institutions – the Young Men's Christian Association. Yes,

I sang "YMCA" by the Village People – mostly because I could spell "YMCA" and no one would be listening to any of the other lyrics. I was fabulous – the Connecticut Yankee doing disco at a Nashville saloon.

But why this story? On Ascension Sunday and Mother's no less. I sang a song in a Nashville honkey-tonk. Me! I did that! I took a risk. I chose to live. I jumped in. Check one off the bucket list. Before that moment, I was just a guy from Connecticut. Now, I'm an aspiring country western singer.

One of our great prophets, William Sloan Coffin once said, "If you choose, you may be wrong. But if you never choose, you are always wrong." Think about those transformative moments in your life, where you were a different person afterwards: a graduation, the birth of your child. But even more so, all those smaller moments which were the real moments of change: the first time you argued a case in a courtroom or taught a lesson in a classroom or drove your parents car all by yourself. We become different people, I believe, when we invest our passion and our love in these moments – like the first time you got the courage to speak the words, "I love you," with another person and really meant it. Transformative stuff.

The story from the Gospel tells how Jesus is raised up into heaven. The story comes after Easter, after the cross, after he comes back to life. It is an uncertain in-between time for the church. Was Jesus the Messiah? Are the teachings true? The disciples are underground.

Jesus is risen, but comes and goes in and out of the disciples' lives. He appears in an upper room when the doors are locked and Thomas puts his hands into the Jesus' side. Jesus appears to two disciples on the road to Emmaus and shares a meal with them. Jesus appears on a beach and tells the disciples how to "fish for all people."

Jesus appears to his disciples in this story. He says to them, "These are my words that I spoke to you while I was still with you – that everything written about me in the law of Moses, the prophets, and the psalms must be fulfilled." Then the passage reads, "Then he opened their minds to understand the scriptures."

That word "open" is very interesting. As I looked into this, there are two words for open in Greek. The first is ἀνοίγω (anooigo) which is the word you would use to open a door. But Jesus uses διανοίγω (dianoigo) that little hook "δια" means, "to break through." The word "to understand" συνίημι (suniemi) means to put all the pieces together, to synthesize all of the facts into one whole. He does not use this word. He uses διανοίγω (dianoigo). Jesus breaks through into their minds so that they finally "get it."

There are two ascensions to this story, two risings. The first is the rising of Jesus Christ into heaven. The second ascension is the rising of his disciples into a new way of being. Their minds have broken through to a new way of understanding. So much so, that it has led their hearts to worship. They are continually in the temple blessing God. They took a risk in following Jesus. They chose to live. They jumped in. They are a transformed people, forever and ever.

Maybe that "breakthrough understanding" has not happened for you yet. I think it appropriate to invoke the wisdom of William Sloan Coffin again who said, "Faith. First you leap. Then you grow wings." I think there is a power in taking a risk, choosing to live, to love, and jumping in. The disciples were humble regular people. The first thing they did: they took that risk.

I just finished reading this fascinating book, How the Irish Saved Civilization, by Thomas Cahill.* It is such a bold title, I was curious about this book for

* Cahill, Thomas. *How the Irish saved civilization*. Vol. 1. Anchor, 2010.

many years. It tells the story of Europe and the church 400, 500 years after Jesus. What had happened during that time is that the Roman Empire had collapsed. Rome was sacked by the Visigoths in 410AD. Around that time, these northern tribes - the Huns, the Gauls, the Goths stormed across Western Europe. Because of all the wars and collapse of culture, the great centers of learning – the early libraries, the early churches, and the fledgling universities – also collapsed. All the great works of classical Greek and Latin literature and philosophy had fallen into obscurity. The early church was also in a state of collapse.

Hope was not lost. In Ireland, Saint Patrick took a risk, chose to live, and jumped in. Saint Patrick is the first missionary who was not an original disciple. As a child, Patrick was captured and sold into slavery. As a young man, he escaped. He did many things, but he was on fire for God – in particular God's power to liberate and the God's care has for least of these – slaves, prisoners, and children.

His early monks realized that literacy was critical for the faith, and so they learned to read the Bible. As they became more literate, they discovered the Greek and Latin literature of the classical period – Plato, Aristotle, Cicero, and Horace. In addition to grappling with these big ideas, they needed to square their faith with their Celtic pagan culture. So, they lived in community. They modeled as best they could a loving monastic community. They copied these ancient books.

These monks – with very earthy names like Columba and Aidan - practiced what they called a white martyrdom. They sailed off into the white sky to mainland Europe to spread the gospel knowing they would have adventure, knowing they would never return. Those monks brought their passion for God along with their Greek and Latin; and they inoculated Europe with the teachings of both. They took a risk. They chose to live, to love, to jump in.

I wonder if, in a very real way, our church functions like an Irish monastery from 1500 years ago. Those early monks incubated their faith, expanded their knowledge, modeled love as best they could, and then went out into the world to share the good news. Those humble monks re-energized the faith for an entire continent and restored an entire canon of Greek and Latin literature. Pretty awesome.

The world is a tough place. The world needs a good church. We are that church. We model as best we can a community of love. We seek an authentic faith that is squared with our intellect. We risk. We choose to live, to love, to jump in.

Will this save our cities? Will this save our country, our world? It is bold to think that we, a humble church, could live out the love of God in such a way. And yet, the Church has already done this very thing at least once before. Why not again? Why not with us? Amen.

Christ's Baptism and Honduran Pizza

In those days Jesus came from Nazareth of Galilee and was baptized by John in the Jordan. And just as he was coming up out of the water, he saw the heavens torn apart and the Spirit descending like a dove on him. And a voice came from heaven, "You are my Son, the Beloved; with you I am well pleased."

And the Spirit immediately drove him out into the wilderness. He was in the wilderness forty days, tempted by Satan; and he was with the wild beasts; and the angels waited on him.

Now after John was arrested, Jesus came to Galilee, proclaiming the good news of God, and saying, "The time is fulfilled, and the kingdom of God has come near; repent, and believe in the good news."

~ MARK 1:9-15

A million years ago, I spent a year as a medical missionary. Around month eleven in my year living overseas, I began to have a powerful hunger for pizza. I would look across that broad, flat, acrid brush of the Miskito flatlands in the back jungles of Honduras, and I would dream of a cheesy, soupy, steamy pie with everything on it. Because I was schooled in New Haven, I began ordering imaginary pizzas from the different establishments around town: a tropical pizza from Modern on State Street, a sausage, onion, garlic, clam pizza from the famous Pepe's, a quick, simple, cheese slice from Yorkside – to go. One desperate day, I took a tortilla, some refried beans, and some ketchup, but it did not look anything like a pizza.

When I stepped off the plane in La Ceiba – a sleepy port town that had the first paved road in a million miles. To my delight, there in the airport, if you can believe it, was a pizza stall. The pizza tasted like the cardboard box it has been sweltering in for the entire day, but pizza never tasted so good.

This is a story about Lent. Lent is a much misunderstood season in the Christian church. Lent is the period of time – 40 days plus Sundays – that precedes Easter. This season in the church calendar is meant to parallel the forty days Jesus spent in the desert

Many folks embrace the tradition of "giving something up for God." Chocolate. Meat. Television. As if what we sacrifice will somehow be registered by God. This is not a bad practice if one can be in touch with the spirituality behind it.

The point to Lent is not how much you can give up, or how disciplined you are. The point to Lent is to know how much you need God, how weak we are, how grateful we ought to be for Christ's presence in our lives.

The amount of chocolate you give up does not compare with what God gave up when his Son died on the cross. If you stop watching TV but it does not deepen your faith or your gratitude to God, then what good is it? If you give up watching American Idol but do not change your life, then what good is it?

When Jesus went into the wilderness and was tempted in the wilderness, he came out with a new message, "The time is fulfilled, and the kingdom of God has come near; repent, and believe in the good news." Jesus came out of his time in the wilderness and he had a new message. He was a person with a new message, a new vision: "Repent, change your lives, believe in the good news."

The purpose to Lent is just that – to become a new person. Indeed, the whole purpose of our faith is to become a new person in Christ, to leave our old selves behind, and to be made whole and holy in Christ.

I am glad that all the New Haven Methodist churches are having a Tuesday evening Lenten series. We shall congregate with one another. And we shall also come together in true faith.

I want to change gears a little bit and talk about why Jesus was baptized and why he was tempted. Lots of folks – diehard Christians, people outside the faith – look at this passage where Jesus was baptized and scratch their heads. "If Jesus did not have sin, why was he baptized?" "If Jesus had no sin, then why did he need to repent?"

Good questions. I have two answers. First, Jesus was baptized not because of the baptism, but because of the dove. The passage from Mark says, "And just as he was coming up out of the water, he saw the heavens torn apart and the Spirit descending like a dove on him. And a voice came from heaven, "You are my Son, the Beloved, with you I am well pleased." (Mark 1:10-11) Jesus was baptized so that God could break open the heavens and reveal who Christ really was.

Second, Jesus was baptized he needed to be baptized. Jesus Christ is fully God and fully human. Jesus Christ needed to make the decision to turn towards his Father. For 30 years, he worked as a carpenter's son building things for other people. On the day of his baptism, he began another type of carpentry. He began building up souls for the kingdom of God.

Before his baptism, he was living a regular life as the good son of Joseph and Mary. When Jesus was baptized he came into his true self as the Son of God, fully God, fully human. The baptismal waters are connected to the Great Flood in the book of Genesis. When God covered the earth with water, and the waters receded, the earth was to begin anew. The earth was "baptized" and was now a new place. The waters of baptism are the same thing: you are made new. The water on the outside points to the change of heart on the inside.

And so we come to Lent to build up our faith. One way in which we lack faith is that we believe the "good news" is not all that great. And so we hedge our bets, don't we. What I am about to say is complicated, so I hope to say it clearly.

In our society, we have higher expectations of ourselves than we do of God. We believe that it is all up to us. We believe that we have to stand alone and show God how tough we are, how holy we are, how much stuff we gave up for Lent. Instead, Lent is to teach us how much we need God.

"The time is fulfilled, and the kingdom of God has come near; repent, and believe in the good news." Amen

A Tradition in Granite and Glass
The Story of Ida Scudder at South Church

When he had gone out, Jesus said, "Now the Son of Man has been glorified, and God has been glorified in him. If God has been glorified in him, God will also glorify him in himself and will glorify him at once. Little children, I am with you only a little longer. You will look for me; and as I said to the Jews so now I say to you, 'Where I am going, you cannot come.' I give you a new commandment, that you love one another. Just as I have loved you, you also should love one another. By this everyone will know that you are my disciples, if you have love for one another."

~ JOHN 13:31-35

Loving, Wonderful God, Thanks be to you for sending your Son the Christ, who spoke words of love and comfort. Move us, God, by these words, by our meditations, our thoughts, our prayers, that we could grow in love for you, and deeper in faith. Bless these words, that they might be yours. In Christ's name, Amen.

I want to share a story about blood and guts, love and betrayal. This is a story about South Church. This is a story about you. This is a true story. Here we go.

The year is 1891. A young girl, the third generation of missionaries, is reading a book on a hot, dreary night in South India. Like any young person, stuck in a back-water, dusty town, her aspiration was to get out of the family business, get out of being a missionary. Get married. Settle down. Someplace cool would be nice.

There is knock on the door. A man is there, urgent, pleading…. "My wife is in labor, and she is having trouble…. Come at once."

She answers, "I am not the doctor, but I will get my father who is."

"No, no," says the man. "A man cannot attend a woman in childbirth."

"Then there is nothing I can do."

And the man slips back into the night.

Some time passes; there is a second knock on the door. Another man is there, urgent, pleading, "My wife is in labor, and she is having trouble…. Come at once."

"I am not the doctor," says the young girl. "But I will get my father who is."

"No, no," says the man. "In our culture, it is taboo for a man to attend a woman in childbirth."

"Then there is nothing I can do."

And the man slips into the darkness.

Unbelievably, there is a third knock on the door. Incredibly, there is a third man at the door, urgent, pleading. "My wife is in labor, and she is having trouble. Come at once."

"But I am not a doctor, and I cannot help you. But I will get my father who is a doctor."

"No," says the man. "In our culture, no man can touch a woman who is in labor…. It is forbidden." And the man slips into the darkness.

In the morning, there is crying in the streets. The young girl learns that three babies and three women have died during the night. What does this story have anything to do with South Church? Stay with me.

So moved by the events of that night, she makes a vow to God that she will do something to help. In 1899, she is the first female graduate of Cornell Medical School.

She returns to India to her family home, and begins delivering babies in the back room of her family home. Two years later, she opens a 40 bed hospital. In 1917, she opens a Medical School for women. In 1947, the medical school goes co-ed. Fast forward to the year 2007, the Vellore Christian Medical Center is the largest Christian hospital in the world. With its rural care program and large hospital, Vellore takes care of 3,000 patients a day (by contrast a place like Yale-New Haven maybe takes care of about 2,000 patients a day).

Now, what does any of this have anything to do with South Church? There are six women immortalized in stained glass in our sanctuary. To my left, in the back, there are the four prominent women of the new testament: Mary, mother of Jesus, Elizabeth, mother of John the Baptist, Mary Magdalene who was at the cross, and Dorcas, a prominent church leader in the book of Acts. All that makes sense. Also to my left, next to St. Augustine, is St. Cecelia, a third century martyr and patron saint of music. This also makes sense.

The sixth woman, and the woman of whom I speak is the Dr. Ida Scudder. The window was placed in memory of Mr. And Mrs. Matthias Sandberg in 1961, one year after Dr. Scudder died.

What kind of church immortalizes a person like Dr. Scudder in their stained glass window? She has no connection to New Britain, CT, no connection to New England. What kind of church bothers to have a missionary window in the first place?

After medical school, I served as a medical missionary in the rural villages of South India, in and around Vellore Christian Medical Center. It was there that I encountered Dr. Ida Scudder's legacy. Imagine the joy when I met her again her at South Church.

Her story is inspiring, for sure, but what I appreciate about her story is that she is human and approachable. She is the only person adorned in our windows who died in the 20th century. Everyone else, died long before. She did not start out to change the world. She started out to care for people. She had courage, faith, patience, perseverance, and love, true love, for what she did, for how else could she have survived so long?

What sort of church emblazons the image of Dr. Ida Scudder in its stained glass? A church with a heart for mission, a church with a tradition of reaching out to those of different cultures and different countries, a church with the courage to take a risk, and to love boldly. Mission is our heritage, our tradition; it is in the glass and granite of this wonderful place. Folks from South Church repaired the home of an elderly couple with Rebuilding Together. And yesterday, brother Merrill organized a group of folks to march on Hartford. And today, we walk for hunger. In my four quick weeks here, I have met the most dedicated, thoughtful bunch of Christians ever. I have met the Ida Scudders of today. I know them by name, for they are you.

I want to change the topic a little bit and talk about love, because that is what our scripture passage was about. We ministers *love* to talk about *love*, but I'm not sure if we do such a great job at it. I think we ministers tend to simplify love – "faith, hope, and love abide, and the greatest of these is love," "God is love," that sort of thing – like the Gospel is some kind of Hallmark card.

I think love is complicated and hard, and here is why: Love is unconditional. In the year 2007, we put all sorts of conditions on our love. In our Desperate-Housewives-Sopranos-Sex-In-The-City sort of love, love is always conditional. It always comes with strings attached. "I will love you if you buy me stuff." "I will love you, for now, while you are good looking." "I will love you, because it fits it fits my lifestyle."

The passage we read looks like a simple, happy, straight-forward saying of Jesus, "I give you a new commandment, that you love one another. Just as I have loved you, you also should love one another" (John 13:34)

It sounds simple enough, straightforward, and non-controversial. But context is everything. This passage came from John chapter 13. In this very same chapter, verse 21, Jesus says, "I tell you the truth, one of you is going to betray me."

"Which one will that be?" asks one of the disciples.

"It is the one to whom I will give this piece of bread when I have dipped it in the dish." Says Jesus. Then, dipping the piece of bread, Jesus gives it to Judas Iscariot, son of Simon.

As soon as Judas took the bread, Satan entered into him. Jesus said to him, "What you are about to do, do quickly."

And Judas Iscariot goes out into the night to alert the temple guards. Judas Iscariot goes out into the night to betray Jesus.

The very next thing that Jesus says is the passage we hear this morning, "Now the Son of Man has been glorified, and God has been glorified in him." (John 13:31) At the instant of his betrayal, Jesus's love is unconditional, unwavering. At the instant when the cascade of events begins that leads to his crucifixion, Jesus's love is unconditional and unwavering.

Every picture I see of Dr. Ida Scudder, shows her smiling. I believe that she was able to connect her love with her action. She served people who were different from her - different religion, different culture, different socio-economic station, everything. She loved her people unconditionally.

Love is hard and messy and painful. But at the end of the day, love is life. Love is power. Love is resurrection. Love is Easter.

I did something last week that I had not yet done before at South Church. I used to do it all the time in New Haven, but last week was my first time as a minister here at South Church: I invited someone to church.

People need many things: healthcare, a good job, a safe place to live, and many things. In addition to all that, I believe that what people need is church. People do not need iPhones or cable TV or Wifi. We *think* we need that stuff, but we do not. People need a home that surrounds their home. People need a sanctuary from the world. People need a place where they can engage the world.

I invited someone to church, and I found it very easy to do, for we have a lot to offer a person looking for a home in this frenetic world so loved by God. We are a church in the tradition of Ida Scudder, a church of missionaries. I put out a challenge for all of us this week: love boldly, without abandon. Invite someone to church. See how it feels. It might easier than you think. Invite someone to church, for we are a church with a tradition of love that is in the granite and glass of this place, this great church. Brothers and Sisters, let us pray…..

The Wounds We Become

Which one of you, having a hundred sheep and losing one of them, does not leave the ninety-nine in the wilderness and go after the one that is lost until he finds it? When he has found it, he lays it on his shoulders and rejoices. And when he comes home, he calls together his friends and neighbors, saying to them, "Rejoice with me, for I have found my sheep that was lost." Just so, I tell you, there will be more joy in heaven over one sinner who repents than over ninety-nine righteous persons who need no repentance.

~ *Luke* 15:4-7

Gracious, Loving God, the prodigal Son found his home again with his Father. So too do we seek our true home with you. May these words, and our meditations help us on our journey. In Christ's name, Amen.

I want to talk about wounds. Emotional wounds. Spiritual wounds. And what to do about these wounds. And I want to use as our template the story of the prodigal son.

Life is hard. We all have wounds that we nurse. We all have scar tissue on our hearts – from past deeds, a bummed out relationships, the job gone south, bad luck.

Now, it has become fashionable, expected perhaps, to have our wounds define who we are as a person. Maybe we get this from talk shows. Maybe from our therapist. Maybe from our friends. So, we say things like,

"I am a recovering addict."

"I am a victim of abuse."
"I am the daughter of an alcoholic."

Susan Sontag, the author of a book of essays called Illness as Metaphor gets at this idea even with the notion of illness.* "I am a cancer patient." "I am a diabetic."

There is a subtle line that one crosses. You might be a person with diabetes, who grew up in a home where your father abused alcohol, and somewhere along the line you started to think of yourself not just as a person wrestling with chronic illness with a past, but rather as "a diabetic and son of an alcoholic."

What happens is that we lose who we are and become our wounds. The illness within us becomes who we are. The brokenness within us becomes what defines us.
"I have bipolar disorder."
"I am a gambler."
"I am an unemployed computer programmer."

The 12-step program – a terrific spiritual revolution in our country – encourages us to say, "Hi, I am Ben. I am a fill-in-the-blank." "Hi, I am Ben. I am a caffeine addict." The 12 step program uses this proclamation as a starting point to your healing, your life does not end there.

The danger, of course, to becoming our wounds is that you lose yourself to your brokenness. The scar of pain in our life holds onto you forever and ever and ever. You become your pain. You become your scar. The human being that you are – made in the image of God, beloved by God – becomes lost to the pain that defines you.

---

* Susan, Sontag. "Illness as Metaphor." *New York, Farrar, Strauss and Giroux* (1978).

In the story of the Prodigal Son, Jesus lays out the story of "a gambler," one who practiced "dissolute living." I love that word "dissolute" which has a lovely, soft Victorian ring to it. The word comes from the same Latin root as "dissolve" and means "loosened up," "dissolved," and in a social context, "indulgent and without restraint."

So, on the street today, we might say the Prodigal Son was a "gambling, womanizer, loser," but from polite pulpits across the country, we just give a wink and say, he is just "dissolute."

So, the Prodigal Son asks for his inheritance from his father, who gives him half of his net worth, heaps it upon his son. His son then takes off to Foxwoods and blows it all on "dissolute" living. The liquor flows. Women flock. The party never ends…. Until one day, he wakes up in a drugged-out haze, and discovers that the party is over. No more money. No more so-called friends. No more parties.

Perhaps the real meaning of "dissolute" really is "dissolved." You become "dissolved." You lose yourself. You become mixed up with all that "dissolute" living, that you lose yourself.

So, he gets the only job that an uneducated, untrained playboy can get. He works as a laborer on a farm. To make matters worse, his boss assigns him to feed the pigs.

When Jesus is telling this story, I can imagine his crowds proclaiming a collective, "Gross!" Pigs as you know are not kosher. To touch them makes you unclean. To serve them makes you lower than the unholy, untouchable, unclean pigs. The prodigal son hits bottom. He sees the dried corn he feeds to the pigs and wishes he could share the meal.

He realizes that the servants of his father have it better off. And so, he heads home to sign on with his father as a servant.

When he arrives home, two interesting things happen. First, he says, "Father I have sinned against heaven and before you; I am no longer worthy to be called your son, treat me like one of your hired hands."

The language here is important. He owns what he has done, "I have sinned," but he does not say, "Hi, I am a gambler." He possesses what he has done, and then he leaves it behind him. He is not a gambler, or even a recovering gambler. He is a son to his father and that is all he is. He returns home. He has left his old life behind. His wounds shaped him, taught him a valuable lesson, and then he cast it aside, embracing him.

The second thing that happens is that his father greets him, embraces him, loves him, not as a gambler-womanizer-dissolver of funds, but rather as his son. The father sees him as he truly is - his son.

Wounds – they must shape us, but not define us. Our pain informs us, but we do not become lost to our pain. We do not become "dissolute" or "dissolved" into our pain.

I want to talk about the wounds of someone else. There was a man who took on the wounds of others, voluntarily. He did not do anything wrong to deserve these wounds, but he bore these wounds out of his love for his brothers and sisters. The wounds that this man Jesus endured were very great – a crown of thorns, nails piercing his hands and feet, a sword in his side, the beatings, the floggings, the humiliation.

Jesus Christ was wounded, but his wounds did not triumph over him. His own death did not swallow him. Those wounds that shaped him, he also left behind.

His wounds are our wounds. His triumph is our triumph. This is the promise of God. Amen.

Faith in a Complicated World

Mary stood weeping outside the tomb. As she wept, she bent over to look into the tomb; and she saw two angels in white, sitting where the body of Jesus had been lying, one at the head and the other at the feet. They said to her, "Woman, why are you weeping?" She said to them, "They have taken away my Lord, and I do not know where they have laid him." When she had said this, she turned around and saw Jesus standing there, but she did not know that it was Jesus. Jesus said to her, "Woman, why are you weeping? Who are you looking for?" Supposing him to be the gardener, she said to him, "Sir, if you have carried him away, tell me where you have laid him, and I will take him away." Jesus said to her, "Mary!" She turned and said to him in Hebrew, "Rabbouni!" (which means Teacher). Jesus said to her, "Do not hold on to me, because I have not yet ascended to the Father. But go to my brothers and say to them, 'I am ascending to my Father and your Father, to my God and your God.'"

~ JOHN *20:11-17*

Holy and Loving God, Mary did not recognize you on that first Easter morning, and so we pray that on this Easter morning, we would recognize you – in these words, in our meditations, in this church. Bless these words that they would be yours. In Jesus' name, Amen.

I want to talk about why Easter matters. Why this day matters. There are so many wonderful traditions around Easter – the colored eggs, the Easter bonnet, the old familiar hymns. In the front yard of our home, we have a giant pink and purple wooden bunny rabbit, 5 feet tall, fang-like teeth about 2 inches long, that says, "Happy Easter." Poppa Joe, my father-in-law, set it up one evening. My wife was thrilled. He said it was an inheritance from Uncle Frankie. What could we say?

So, why does Easter matter? I believe that Easter is important. In fact, I believe that Easter is the most important thing that has ever happened to my life, your life, or for the entire world. To get at why Easter is so important, I want to talk about the world we live in – your life and mine. Then, I want to talk about Jesus – what he *shows* us and what he *does* for us.

First, the world. When I work in the hospital at night, every night, the Emergency Room fills with people with no place to go – drug addicts stoned out of their minds, alcoholics shackled to the gurney, smelling of vomit, people wrestling with demons and voices in their head with no place to go, and often homeless people with no place to go, too cold to sleep outdoors. We live in the wealthiest country at the wealthiest time in history. We are the only super-power. In such a country, why are there so many people on the margins. Why is the poverty so great? Why is there so much despair? Why do so many, many people cry, "How long, O Lord, how long?"

Sadly, we live in a world of lies upon lies upon lies where the rich and the powerful seem to have the upper hand. We are a country at war. And no one is sure why. There is political back-peddling and smoke screens. Who can you trust in this world? Your doctors? The ones who order all those tests so they won't get sued? Your politicians? I won't even go there. Your clergy? I wish we had a more pristine reputation.

Why do you wake up in the morning with a pit of despair and sorrow in your life? You have all you need – cable TV, a cell phone, and all the accouterments of modern life. Where does this searing pain of loneliness, the chronic nagging guilt, why have you not measured up to all the dreams that you have dreamt for yourself? Could it be that our country is misguided? Could it be that our society is misguided? Could it be that you are misguided?

William Sloane Coffin, an old preacher and peace activist from down the road, once said, "We crucify the best *among* us, because we crucify the best *within* us."* We are dominated by what we have been – our mistakes, our guilt, our family burden – rather than by what we can become.

The world is a tough place. And when we get tough in face of the world, our heart closes. We close ourselves off from love. We close ourselves off from how God can touch us.

And then Jesus comes to startle us awake, to shakes us to our senses, from our numbing, hard lives to say, "There is something more. There is something better. There is life. There is love."

And when Jesus breaks into our shell to reveal what we have truly become, we crucify him in the time-honored tradition of the king who kills the messenger of bad news. That is why Jesus was crucified – because he showed us what we have become. We are dominated by our past – our past sin, our guilt, our depression – all the things that hold us back. We are dominated by what we have been, rather than what we can become.

Jesus does two things. He *shows* us something and he *does* something. I am humbled to stand in a pulpit on Easter Sunday. I stand here not as a prophet, but as a humble man, a father, a husband, who wrestles with the demons of guilt and suffering and doubt like all of us do. I stand here, like you do, at the edge of an empty tomb, hopeful – could it be

---

* Coffin, William Sloane. *Living the Truth in a World of Illusions*. HarperCollins Publishers, 1985, page 52.

35

true? – that this man Jesus is in fact the Christ. Could the man Jesus be the Christ?

"Whom are you looking for?" says the Gardener.

"The Lord," we reply.

And there is a small whisper, a silent voice, a clear bell in the distance. It is the whisper of faith, "It is true." Can you hear it in your heart? "It is true."

Jesus shows us that death is not the tragedy in our lives. Death is not the tragedy. The tragedy of our lives is the million little deaths that build up over time – the missed opportunities to love and be loved. Death is not the tragedy, but a life not fully lived – that is the tragedy.

Just to be alive is such a miracle. I look at my children, any child really, and they are so beautiful, so perfect, and so precious. To inspire the clean, fresh spring air, a miracle. We start out so well, don't we?

In our life, which is such a miracle, if we can have an inkling of faith and hope to guide our lives. A tiny bit of faith and hope is such a great comfort, such a gift.

So, our lives are a miracle, and God help us, if we can have faith and hope, but yet, we were made for something more weren't we? We are made to love. In addition to the miracle of being alive, and the great gift of hope and faith, embracing all that, if we can know true love in our lives, that is a great gift indeed – it is an Easter gift.

Jesus died so that we would have this great love. We have all manner of platitudes – "Jesus died to set us free" "Jesus died for our sins." "Jesus is the lamb of God who takes away the sin of the world."

It is hard to wrap your mind around such bold claims. If you have trouble with Jesus and resurrection, let me put it another way. Jesus was stronger than death. Jesus was stronger than doubt. Jesus is stronger than your vanity, your pride, your guilt, your illness, your brokenness. You might think that you are so evil, so horrible, that God could never forgive you – but that is simply not true.

When that rock rolled away from that tomb, and the tomb was empty, a whole new way of living came into the world. "It is true" "It is true"

Jesus shows us that there is no victory more important than the triumph of love – but we defeat all chances of this triumph because we fear failure more than we love life. We deny our faith by not daring to live beyond our own egos. Paradise is less a future promise, then a present possibility.

Jesus shows us that death is not the tragedy of our lives, and that there is no greater triumph than the victory of love, but Jesus does something for us as well. Jesus fulfills a prophecy, a prophecy that is throughout scripture. From Isaiah, "On this mountain the Lord of hosts will make for all peoples a feast of rich food…. And he will destroy on this mountain the shroud that is cast over all peoples, the sheet that is spread over all nations; he will swallow up death forever. Then the Lord God will wipe away the tears from all faces, and the disgrace of his people he will take away from all the earth…. It will be said on that day, 'Lo, this is our God, for whom we have waited, let us be glad and rejoice in his salvation.'" (Isaiah 25:6-9)

Jesus lives. And so you live. Forever. The holy love that overwhelms all evil, overcomes all suffering, is the holy love that Christ offers you.

Christ looked different after his resurrection. Mary did not recognize him. His disciples at first did not recognize him. Something was different about him. And that's what resurrection will do. That is what new life, God's love, will do: God will change you and make you new. "Lo, this I sour God, for whom we have waited, let us be glad and rejoice in his salvation." Amen.

The Next Day

When it was evening on that day, the first day of the week, and the doors of the house where the disciples had met were locked for fear of the Jews, Jesus came and stood among them and said, "Peace be with you." After he said this, he showed them his hands and his side. Then the disciples rejoiced when they saw the Lord. Jesus said to them again, "Peace be with you. As the Father has sent me, so I send you." When he had said this, he breathed on them and said to them, "Receive the Holy Spirit. If you forgive the sins of any, they are forgiven them; if you retain the sins of any, they are retained."

~ JOHN 20:19-23

Wonderful, Holy God, Jesus breathes the Holy Spirit upon us so that we might know and believe what Jesus has in store for us. Bless these moments, bless these words, and bless our meditations, that we would know you the more with our hearts and our minds. In Christ's name, Amen.

I want to talk about the Sunday after Easter. If you look at the other major religions of the world, there is a big difference between Jesus and how the other religions' leaders died.

If you look at the Buddha, he died a quiet, peaceful death, surrounded by his followers. If you look at Muhammad, he died a king on earth, having brought liberation and light to a vast land. Now Moses did not get to enter the Promised Land, but he did die just east of the Jordan River as his life's work – the liberation of the Hebrew people – came to fruition.

All of those religious leaders knew respect and admiration and even awe from their communities. All of those religious leaders had the sense of peace and resolution of a life well-lived.

Jesus, on the other hand, died a death of shame and humiliation. Nailed to a cross, half naked, while his mother watched, a good boy from Nazareth, executed as a traitor against the state. He suffered greatly. But more than that, he knew the suffering that only comes from shame and humiliation. The Romans mocked him, "Look at the king of Jews." The tore off his cloak and gambled for it. He suffered the rejection of his own people. The very people who cheered "Hosanna" on Palm Sunday were the people who shouted, "Crucify him" the very next week.

The movement of liberation and freedom and redemption that he founded became completely unraveled. Betrayed by one of his own. His followers fled, living furtively behind locked doors, afraid to be seen in public.

The beginnings of our faith are humble and bloody. But the world is bloody and violent, filled with suffering. Our faith meets us in the muck and mire and struggle of our own lives. Our God walks the bitter path of suffering and shame. Our Christ knows how hard it is to change a human heart. Our Christ know the pain that comes from true love that is lost.

A patient of mine who has used drugs for a long time – he snorted heroin for years – said to me recently with great insight, "I haven't used drugs in 6 months. But yet, I still feel like an addict.... I've been doing all the right things, but I don't yet have my redemption."

The tough part about addiction is that the addiction demon does not fully go away. You can do the right things, but only until the whole person changes, they whole spiritual-psycho make-up of a person.

I believe the only way a person with addictions can truly change is to have a spiritual conversion, a spiritual insight. The addict must put their fingers into the side of the wounded Christ, the living Christ, and say, "My Lord, my God." You are risen. You are risen indeed.

The new life in Christ must become more compelling than the numbing sleep and slow death of drugs. The new life in Christ must become more powerful and real than the shame and depression that the drugs are trying to alleviate.

Life is hard, shame and humiliation and inadequacy are all part of it. But God's power to redeem can lift us higher than our shame. God's love is deeper than the abyss of our suffering.

I believe that people can have a moment when they are "born again," where this understanding happens all at once. That is absolutely valid for me. Yet, I also believe that it limits God that it *must* happen all at once. I also believe that revelation can happen softly, behind a locked door, in the upper room like it happened that first Easter.

I imagine those first disciples were embarrassed. They all fled for their lives. Peter denied Jesus three times. They all wondered what it all meant. The first Easter was quiet and private. No parades. No fanfares of victory. Resurrection was personal and intimate and real.

> "Put your finger in my wounds and see my hands. Reach out your hand and put it in my side. Do not doubt but believe."
> Thomas answered him, "My Lord and my God."
> Jesus says, "Have you believed because you have seen me? Blessed are those who have not seen and yet have come to believe?"

Maybe you are not addicted to heroin. Maybe you have other demons squeezing your heart. Maybe you feel like you just don't matter, that you have thought about suicide, that you believe the world would be better off without you. This is simply not true. Jesus died on the cross for your redemption, so that you would not have to die a horrible suffering death.

Maybe you wrestle with depression, or feel the special embarrassment of unemployment – "Why can't I find something to do?" Our society is not kind to such people. Maybe you were abused either as a child or an adult. One study showed that among a clinic population, 1/3 of people had post-traumatic stress disorder. We think of depression, but PTSD is more than that. It's the depression and anxiety that comes from abuse, a special kind of hell. Life is hard out there.

Maybe you feel like Easter has not happened for you yet. You would be glad to have that "My Lord, My God" experience of Thomas, but it hasn't happened yet. Let me proclaim this, "The Christ who died for you, the Christ who lives for you still, is the Christ who hopes for you, breathes upon you, 'Come Holy Spirit.'" You do not need to be strong enough – indeed we often get in the way of God's work. Your strength is Christ's strength. Your hope is Christ's hope.

God's power to redeem can lift us higher than our shame. God's love is deeper than the abyss of our suffering. Let this be the truth about Easter than heartens us and carries us forward, that we all might be renewing our faith every day, that we all might proclaim together, "My Lord, and My God." Let us pray....

Suffering

The Son Who Did Not Return

The father said to him, "Son, you are always with me, and all that is mine is yours. But we had to celebrate and rejoice, because this brother of yours was dead and has come to life; he was lost and has been found."

~ *Luke 15:31-32*

SANDY HOOK & LAMENT FOR A SON
It is a Friday morning, several of us on the Yale medical school faculty are gathering to interview applicants who have traveled across the country to interview for a spot at the residency program. We are milling about.

At 9:40am, my dear friend and colleague receives an automated text page on her cell phone saying that there is a lock-down at her children's elementary school. "There are always lock-downs for one thing or another. Once it was because a fox walked across the play ground," she told me later. "At first, I didn't think much of it."

The day is December 14th. The school is Sandy Hook Elementary. And my dear friend flees back to Newtown to the fire station, not certain if her children are dead or alive. She has two children – a daughter in 3rd grade, and a son in kindergarten. Thank God she found them alive, grief stricken, shaken up, but alive. But too many of her neighbors and close friends lost their children on that day.

She, her husband, and I have been friends for almost 15 years. We spoke often in the days that followed, including a late night session around the kitchen table. There were a lot of scary things that happened that didn't come out in the papers.

What do you say to a friend who does not have enough time in the week to go to all the funerals? Familiar words of comfort seemed so hollow. A faith that I felt sure was bedrock suddenly felt like sand. God, where were you? I don't want to hear about angels in heaven, or some well-crafted explanation about free will. All of it felt so empty.

In my life as a physician, I see a lot of death. In the emergency room, I thump on my patient's chest; I administer shocks; I insert all manner of tubes to ventilate, drain blood, and give strong medicine. When appropriate, I order the morphine to allow a natural death. Death has become not the enemy as much as a familiar, professional colleague, always standing nearby, always with an unnerving opinion. And yet, Sandy Hook just felt so different from all of that.

For so many, it is a grief that lingers like old snow. Where is God amidst this long winter? Where is God amidst all of this grief and doubt and blood? Will spring ever come? When and how will our deliverance come?

I was deeply shaken by it all. And so, I sought out people wiser than I. I read the book of Job in great detail. I poured through books about suffering written by Jews, Baptists and Buddhists, Calvinists and Catholics. My favorite was written by a Yale Divinity School theology professor named Nicholas Wolterstorff. Almost 30 years ago, his 25 year old son died in a rock climbing accident in Austria. Professor Wolterstorff captured his grief in a book called Lament for a Son. I was curious about what he would say: I remember him as a thoughtful, brilliant, clear-headed scholar. Surely, he could set me straight.

He writes about his son, but he could be writing about Sandy Hook, or any other horrible tragedy:

"How is faith to endure, O God, when you allow all this scraping and tearing on us? You have allowed rivers of blood to flow, mountains of suffering to pile up, sobs to become humanity's song – all without lifting a finger that we could see. You have allowed bonds of love beyond number to be painfully snapped. If you have not abandoned us, explain yourself."*

The book is an outpouring of heartfelt grief, which I found so honest, with very little in the way of theology or explanation. I think Professor Wolterstorff understands that the point of grief is to grieve, and not just hurriedly explain it all away. The point of sadness is to be sad and not bury the sadness beneath a truck load of stuffed animals.

THE PRODIGAL SON

Amidst the doubt and grief of Sandy Hook Elementary School, we read the familiar story of the prodigal son, the lost son, with new eyes. *Of course* the father runs towards the Son. Thank God that that the son is alive. *Of course* the father prepares the great celebration. The son was certainly dead, and now is alive.

There are many wonderful cultural details to this story that the original hearers would readily understand. This is a parable - a story that Jesus tells to illustrate a point of how God works in the world. It is not a parable about how to raise children, for example. I want to raise up the three characters in this story.

First, the prodigal son, the young son. When the son asks for his inheritance from the father, it is the ultimate insult. Then, like now, you receive your inheritance when your father dies. More than that, in the Middle Eastern culture of the time, to receive your inheritance means to receive land. How much land you had is tied into your social standing and future security. The word that is used in this passage is *bios* – life. The prodigal son is asking

---

* Wolterstorff, Nicholas. *Lament for a Son*. Wm. B. Eerdmans Publishing, 1987, page 80.

his father to tear apart his land, his life, and give his life over to his son. To ask for your inheritance is to say to the father, "You are now dead to me."

The second cultural piece is about the older son. Everyone knows this story as the "prodigal son," but that's not how Jesus tells the story. Jesus begins the story, "A man had two sons." To leave out the older son is to miss a really important part of this parable. The older "good" son has a lot more in common than one might think with the young "bad" son.

When the younger brother returns, the older son is enraged. "I've worked like a slave for you all these years, and you've never once gave me even a goat." The older son disrespects his father, refuses to go into the family feast. The older "good" son and the younger "prodigal" son are the same in this one respect: they both squander the father's love. They want his stuff. They do not want his love.

The third detail is about the father. The father loves them both despite themselves. The father runs towards the son and kisses him. Patriarchs do not run. Children run. Soldiers run. Patriarchs do not run. The inferior approaches the superior. Also, patriarchs do not kiss. The inferior kisses the superior as a sign of respect. The father in this story does not do that. This father runs towards the lost son and kisses him. The father says, "put the best robe upon him and the ring on his finger." The ring is the signet ring, the ring by which the patriarch would sign contracts and represent the family.

Jesus is telling us about how God works. We might believe that God is dead to us. We might live as if God is absent from our lives – and we all know it is so easy to do that. Jesus tells us that God will run to you, reach out for you, ache for you, kiss you, tear his life apart for you, suffer for you, and love you.

LOVE AND SUFFERING

I love the question that Nicholas Wolterstorff asks God, "If you have not abandoned us, explain yourself." Later in the book, he attempts an answer. He writes,

"We strain to hear. But instead of hearing an answer, we catch sight of God himself scraped and torn. Through our tears, we see the tears of God."* "God is love. That is why he suffers. To love our suffering sinful world is to suffer.... The one who does not see God's suffering does not see his love. God is suffering love...."† "We are in it together, God and we, together in the history of our world. The history of our world is the history of our suffering together. Every act of evil extracts a tear from God, every plunge into anguish extracts a sob from God. But the history of our world is the history of our deliverance together. God's work to release himself from his suffering is his work to deliver the world from its agony; our struggle for joy and justice is our struggle to relieve God's sorrow."*

To love is to suffer. Every parent understands that. Anyone who has ever loved understands that. And in this love is our deliverance and our very life.

The world is so violent, so tragic, and so beautiful too. We rage against the injustice of it all and suffer our grief. When we do this, we become the incarnation of God's love for the world. In our loving and suffering, we discover the loving, suffering Christ who tears apart his *bios*, his life. In our suffering love, we encounter the Christ who draws us to him in hope, in healing, in deliverance. This is the promise of God. Amen.

---

* Wolterstorff, *Lament for a Son*, page 80.
† Wolterstorff, *Lament for a Son*, page 90.
* Wolterstorff, *Lament for a Son*, page 91.

"They Stole Our Tears"

The days are surely coming, says the Lord, when I will make a new covenant with the house of Israel and the house of Judah. It will not be like the covenant that I made with their ancestors when I took them by the hand to bring them out of the land of Egypt—a covenant that they broke, though I was their husband, says the Lord. But this is the covenant that I will make with the house of Israel after those days, says the Lord: I will put my law within them, and I will write it on their hearts; and I will be their God, and they shall be my people. No longer shall they teach one another, or say to each other, "Know the Lord," for they shall all know me, from the least of them to the greatest, says the Lord; for I will forgive their iniquity, and remember their sin no more.

~ JEREMIAH *31:31-34*

And the Lord said, "Listen to what the unjust judge says. And will not God grant justice to his chosen ones who cry to him day and night? Will he delay long in helping them? I tell you, he will quickly grant justice to them. And yet, when the Son of Man comes, will he find faith on earth?"

~ LUKE *18:6-8*

Holy God, you make a new covenant with us that we would be your people, and you would be our God. Bless these words and our meditations that your promise to us would be our comfort and our strength. In Christ's name we pray, Amen.

Our passage from Luke this morning talks about perseverance and prayer, but one line leaps out, "And will God not grant justice to his chosen ones who cry to him day and night?" There is that word – justice. The word justice is ultimately a political word.

I want to talk about justice, and in particular, politics. Among polite, classy, enlightened people – people like you and I - there are four things that we never discuss in public: sex, money, politics, and religion. Here at South Church no topic is taboo. This morning: religion and politics.

There are two camps in the church. The first camp says that religion and politics should be separate. Religion is about my soul, my behavior, my relationship with God. Religion is private. The government does not interfere with my church. My church ought not interfere in my government.

Wise people will point out that the church is a tax-exempt institution and we should do nothing to threaten that. Let the church be a community of morality, but let us not inflict our views upon the rest of the world. This position has a very strong American sensibility, and is all about the freedom of expression and the separation of church and state.

The other side says that religion must be political. Religion must be enmeshed, embroiled in the political scene. Look what God does with the people of Israel when they were slaves: God sets them free. Look what Jesus does in the temple when he casts out the money-changers. Look at the liberation theologians. Look at the peace marches of William Sloane Coffin. To be religious, you must be politically active.

That is the spectrum – more or less. Keep religion and politics completely separate or fuse them together. I have a lot of thoughts about this, but to help us wrestle with this, I want to tell you a story, a true story. Here it goes:

As many of you know, for my other gig during the week, I am the medical director of a clinic within the Yale Empire up in Waterbury, CT. It is the clinic for the medicine-pediatrics residency program where the residents and faculty see their patients.

It is August of this year in this very special place when the story begins. Dr. Joan Jasien, a third-year resident, comes to me to present a patient. You've seen how this works on TV. The resident physician presents a patient to the wise and wizened, slightly gray-haired physician-professor. The attending physician makes a few wise comments and breezes on.

In the crowd where I run, I am lucky if I'm a paragraph ahead. In any case, Dr. Jasien comes out of the exam room. There is a ring of excitement in her voice and the exchange is completely different. "There is a family here from Burma. They are refugees. They have been placed here by a special government program."

There is a kind-faced college-kid-social-work-intern named Dan. He has a thick notebook with lots of papers sticking out of it. "We have 40 refugees from the Karen tribe of Burma – the government calls themselves Myanmar these days. More refugees are coming. I've been trying to find doctors for the families, but no one wants to take care of them. They are complicated, and they don't speak a word of English."

Before that common-sense-rational-part of the brain kicked in, the passionate-fire-in-the-belly-jump-first-ask-questions-later side of the brain suspected that there might be angels about. I heard myself say, "We shall care for all of them. We shall be the doctors for all them."

What happened next has captured the passions of our team. We made a house call with 7 doctors and a nurse. We vaccinated everyone, treated parasites, took care of all that medical stuff. We learned how to says things like, "Nay lo kathari tsa a?" "Do you have a headache?" "Nay lo moco tsa a?" "Do you have a runny nose?"

My name fortunately can be translated into almost any language. In the Karen language, I am Dr. Ma Chichi.

We wanted to learn more. We convened a dinner with several of the Karen-folk and their Karen-Burmese social worker. We wanted to hear their story. We learned that Burma is a country east of India, with China on it's northern border, and Thailand to the south. We learned that the Karen people live in the forested hills on the Burmese-Thai border. We learned that they are farmers; they grow rice and keep pretty much to themselves. They are a minority: they speak their own language, and have their own traditions.

We learned that the government is a military dictatorship. They changed the name to Myanmar to reflect the dominant ethnic group. The name Myanmar would be like calling the United States of America, "Caucasian-land."

Because the Karen are a minority, and because of the land they occupy, the military dictatorship seeks to exterminate them. The militia burn their rice crops so that the Karen starve. The militia enslaves the men to build roads. They do horrible things to the women and the girls. They are brutal with any uprising.

The Karen people flee from all this. They head up into the mountains and hide in caves. They seek refuge across the border in Thailand. The Thai government does not recognize them, so the Karen people live their lives in fear, adrift, constantly on the move, vigilant, in a chronic state of panic.

What a young man said on that night was particularly striking, "When we hid from the soldiers, my mother would poke me with a stick, and I would clench my jaw, so that I would not cry. As children, we were never allowed to cry, because that could reveal our hiding place. I would never cry. I did not want to the army to find me, to find my family. The soldiers stole my tears."

"What did you say?" I asked, "That last part again?"

"They stole my tears."

He is right. When we vaccinate the children. They never cry. They stare straight ahead, stone silent, and they do not cry. Their tears have been stolen. Their childhood has been stolen. Their home has been stolen. They do not cry. Their tears have been stolen.

Our Lord Jesus says, "And will not God grant justice to his chosen ones who cry out to him day and night?"

Why do I tell this story about a far away hill tribe? This story has been played over and over again in the world: in East Timor in the 1990's, in the United States among Native Americans in the 19th century and the Japanese during WWII, in Nazi Germany, in Somalia in our present day, and on and on. We live in a world where the strong inflict their will upon the weak; where the oppressed cry out, "How long, O Lord, how long?"

There is another hill tribe who suffered the oppression of a stronger power. They too asked the question, "How long, O Lord, how long?" The prophet Jeremiah answers the people of Israel, "This is the covenant that I will make with the house of Israel after those days, says the LORD: I will put my law within them, and I will write it on their hearts; and I will be their God, and they shall be my people."

This is a spiritual claim, but it is also a promise of redemption and restoration. When Jeremiah spoke those words, the Babylonians had invaded Israel. Soon, the Babylonians would lay siege to Jerusalem. In the year 586 BC, the Babylonians crush Israel. They march the Israel's strong and rich to Babylon to live out their days as slaves. Only a remnant of the weak and old remain behind to tend the ruins of God's Kingdom on earth.

God promises to be their God at their darkest hour, at the moment of their greatest defeat. "This is the covenant that I will make with the house of Israel after those days…I will put my law within them, and I will write it on their hearts; and I will be their God, and they shall be my people."

I realize now that doctoring a Burmese refugee is political. In its most graphic, literal terms, if a soldier wants to shoot my patient, and I want my patient to live, does that soldier want to shoot me? Am I am enemy of the Myanmar government?

I realize now that being a Christian in this world cannot help but be political. Religion *is* political. Just by being here in this sanctuary, at this hour, we make a statement. Just by being here, we take a stand against hatred, against materialism. If we stand with Christ, we stand with the ones on the outside, and we bring them to the table. If we stand at the cross, we claim that love is stronger than evil.

The powerful inflict their will upon the weak. The weak cry out, and who shall hear them but us? Who shall be the prophet Jeremiah for our age? Who but us? Who but the church?

The world is a hard place where the strong inflict their will upon the weak. Yet, we are the people of God's promise, and in this, there is hope and power.

One of our patients, when she arrived in this country, was full with child. When the baby was born – a beautiful, perfect little boy – my good friend Dr. Richard Shea had the privilege of welcoming this first Karen-American infant.
He asks through an interpreter, "What is your baby's name?"
The mother says in English, "No name. You name the baby."
He says, "I can't name your baby. That's for you to do. It's your baby."
The father says, "You name the baby. You. You. You."

Dr. Shea reflects for a moment. He asks, "Well, what is your religion?"

They say, "Christian."

He says, "Let his name be Christopher."

I ask him later, "Brother Richard, do you realize what the name Christopher means?"

"Of course," he says. "Christopher. The One Who Bears Christ."

Christopher. The One Who Bears Christ.

Christopher. The One Who Bears Christ.

We are the ones who bear Christ in a struggling world. We are the people of the new covenant with God. In this covenant, there is hope and comfort and power.

"And suddenly there was a multitude of the heavenly host praising God and saying, "Glory to God in the highest, and on earth, peace and good will toward all people." (Luke 2:13-14) Amen.

Longing

When they had come near Jerusalem and had reached Bethphage, at the Mount of Olives, Jesus sent two disciples, saying to them, "Go into the village ahead of you, and immediately you will find a donkey tied, and a colt with her; untie them and bring them to me. If anyone says anything to you, just say this, 'The Lord needs them.' And he will send them immediately." This took place to fulfill what had been spoken through the prophet, saying, "Tell the daughter of Zion, Look, your king is coming to you, humble, and mounted on a donkey, and on a colt, the foal of a donkey."

The disciples went and did as Jesus had directed them; they brought the donkey and the colt, and put their cloaks on them, and he sat on them. A very large crowd spread their cloaks on the road, and others cut branches from the trees and spread them on the road. The crowds that went ahead of him and that followed were shouting,

"Hosanna to the Son of David! Blessed is the one who comes in the name of the Lord!

Hosanna in the highest heaven!" When he entered Jerusalem, the whole city was in turmoil, asking, "Who is this?" The crowds were saying, "This is the prophet Jesus from Nazareth in Galilee."

~ MATTHEW *21:1-11*

oving and Wonderful God, speak to us in this place, in the calming of our minds, and in the longing of our hearts, by the words of these lips, and by the thoughts we shape. Speak to us Lord, that these words may be yours. In Christ's name, Amen.

One of the saddest moments I have had as a doctor came earlier this week. It is a story so sad, I almost decided not to tell it, for fear that I would weep (again) from this pulpit. This is a story that has figured large in my life this week, and so when I sharpen my pencil, and prepare for the sermon, I could not shake the story of this little boy – Jonathan (not his real name) – who came into clinic earlier this week. And yet, this story speaks to the world we live in, the struggles we face, the journey that we are on together. It is a holy story.

I have known this little boy Jonathan since his birth. His mother was addicted to crack cocaine, but she brought him regularly for his checkups. His mother loved this little boy, but life overwhelmed her: there were addictions and demons, the sorts of which are hard to imagine.

And so she went off, this struggling woman, to wrestle with her afflictions. The infant Jonathan fell into the state system, foster care, a couple of families, a change here. He kept coming for his checkups, a beautiful boy, big almond eyes, tousled Norman Rockwell hair.

Then God brought Louise into his life. Louise was his foster mom, but she loved him, she really, really loved him. There were rumors of adoption, and then the official paperwork fell across by desk. And there were meetings, and more paperwork. Louise would fill me in on how it was going. And then there was a Christmas card with young Jonathan on the front. And then there was the adoption, an officially stamped, codified, registered rebirth. Jonathan was a little boy again with a mother who loved him, who really loved him.

God has a plan that I do not yet know, for Jonathan's mom fell ill. Cancer. Quickly, too quickly, she died. At the age of 6, Jonathan has lost his second mother. It has been four months or so since she died, and Jonathan is in counseling, with a new foster mom, who is kind to him. Jonathan came in with a cold, a simple cold, a runny nose, a cough, a bit thinner than he should be, but hanging on.

I speak to him, "How are you Jonathan?"

He begins to cry, this frail boy, so sad to the world. He begins to cry, "I want my mommy."

And then I begin to cry. He cries. I cry. His foster mom cries. What is this world, that a boy would lose two mothers in six years? What is this world that an innocent child would know such bone-crushing, soul twisting grief? This little boy loved the way only a child could love, and the world betrayed that love.

Today, he weeps, and carries his grief, his cross. Young Jonathan is utterly and completely alone in the world.

Jonathan's story is not over, and I am confident that he will find his true home, that his grief will abate, that his loneliness will be eased. But his story shines a light on the loneliness and sadness of the world.

I think of the children in Iraq who have lost their parents. I think of the children in New Haven who have no safe place to call home. I think of the children who never knew a parent's love. And what of you and me? What do you carry in your heart? Have you known the loneliness of losing someone you love? What did that feel like?

Our faith is not an intellectual exercise. Our faith is not about a pleasant conversation and a cup of coffee. Our faith is not only the familiar hymn on a happy morning. Our faith is about this man Jesus and what happened this week in Jerusalem. Jesus knows the betrayal of friends and the loss of loved ones.

Tradition has it that "Jesus arrived in Jerusalem like a King." Indeed, I have said the very thing from this very pulpit. But, when I really think about it, Jesus did not arrive like a king. A king would have an entourage, a legion of soldiers in gleaming steal. A king would have had flags and shields and trumpets and dancers. A king would have made an entrance.

No, Jesus did not enter as a king. I think instead, he arrived the way a college kid arrives home on vacation – no, no, that's not right. Jesus arrives in Jerusalem the way a soldier arrives home from war. The crowd is there to greet him, to celebrate who he is, cry out their praises, but then they quickly forget him. The press casts Jesus in a different light, and a few days later, they cry out, "Crucify him! Crucify him!"

Jesus knows the suffering and loneliness of rejection. This week, his people reject him. "Crucify him! Crucify him!" they cry. His friends reject him. "Could you not stay up with me in this Garden of Gethsemane?" "Peter, by the time the rooster crows, you shall have denied me three times."

He even knows the loneliness from God. When he is on the cross, he cries out, "My God, My God, why have you forsaken me?" (Psalm 22) It is not his line, but rather a line from Psalm 22. He could have said many other lines from the psalms, "I lift mine eyes to the hills, from whence does my help come. My help comes in the name of the Lord who made heaven and the earth," Psalm 121 might have been my pick. Good old Psalm 23 would have been a comfort: "The Lord is my shepherd, I shall not want. He leads me beside still waters." Another Psalm would have worked as well, "Out of the depths I cry to you, O Lord. O Lord, hear my voice." (Psalm 130)

But Jesus cries out, "My God, My God, why have your forsaken me?" (Psalm 22)

Jesus knows the loneliness and suffering of being truly alone. Jesus knows the broken-heart of a six year old who has lost his mother. Jesus knows the dark night of the soul. Jesus knows rejection and loss and disgrace. Where does it end?

It ends and begins on the cross. And there we point to our help and our hope. When all appears lost, it is not lost completely. Just when goodness appears to lose to the devil, God's power triumphs. God's love transforms.

We might feel completely and utterly alone, but because Christ rose, we are never completely alone. We are always loved. Even in the dark night of your soul, even sweltering in the desert of your grief, you are embraced by a loving God who does not let you go.

Love is sometimes like flying, and sometimes love is like falling. When you come into this church, and hear these words, and reflect upon what they mean, you invite God's power into your life. You put yourself at risk. You put yourself to risk loving this world, loving the stranger, and loving this magnificent God who calls you to holiness.

Let the suffering of this world be healed with God's touch. Let the loneliness of this world be transformed with the fellowship of Christ. Let us all be instruments of his resurrection. In Christ's name, Amen.

Hope Hemorrhaging

Now there was a woman who had been suffering from hemorrhages for twelve years. She had endured much under many physicians, and had spent all that she had; and she was no better, but rather grew worse. She had heard about Jesus, and came up behind him in the crowd and touched his cloak, for she said, "If I but touch his clothes, I will be made well." Immediately her hemorrhage stopped; and she felt in her body that she was healed of her disease. Immediately aware that power had gone forth from him, Jesus turned about in the crowd and said, "Who touched my clothes?" And his disciples said to him, "You see the crowd pressing in on you; how can you say, 'Who touched me?'" He looked all around to see who had done it. But the woman, knowing what had happened to her, came in fear and trembling, fell down before him, and told him the whole truth. He said to her, "Daughter, your faith has made you well; go in peace, and be healed of your disease."

~ Mark 5:25-34

Loving God, we hear your gospel in hope – could your healing power for them, be healing power for us? Bless these words, and our meditations, that you might be present to us, that we might know your love and healing in our lives. In Christ's name, Amen.

I lost a patient last week. Actually, she never became my patient exactly. The paramedics called in to say that there had been a fight between two women. There were knives. A woman was stabbed twice in the chest.

When the paramedics arrived, there was no pulse. When she arrived in the ER, there was nothing to do but make the pronouncement.

The family arrived, and there was wailing and grief. Police everywhere. Tears choked back by staff. It was all so terribly sad.

There was a double tragedy. There was the horrible, violent death of this young woman, who was a mother to her son. That was the first tragedy. The second tragedy was that there was a complete lack of moral outrage. In the papers the next day, the story merited a paragraph. The following day, when the police arrested the alleged murderer, there was another paragraph. After that, the pages were filled with the next tragedy.

Maybe that is to be expected. There is so much violence in the world there are not enough pages in the newspaper to contain it all. And yet it is all so terribly sad.

Forgive me in sharing this gruesome story. When reflecting about the bleeding woman in our scripture passage, it is impossible to let go of the bleeding woman in the Emergency Room. The two women have a lot in common. For one thing, they both have no name. While this isn't completely true, as far as the world is concerned, what happened on the night of June 21st is quite literally yesterday's news. The two women has suffered greatly in their lives.

I share this story to highlight that what we do as church is so important. Amidst so much that seems hopeless and overwhelming, we are a sanctuary of hope. To worship together on a glorious summer morning gives witness to the world that grace is possible and love is real despite what we read in the papers.

I want to talk about this hemorrhaging woman in our scripture passage. I want to think about three aspects. First, I want to talk about who she was; second, what her faith was; and third, who she was to Jesus.

First, who was this woman? There are a lot of people that Jesus heals who do not have a name: people afflicted with leprosy, paralysis and blindness. And she is one. Whenever Jesus heals someone without a name, it usually means the person did not have a high station in society. This is certainly true here. What is powerful about these nameless people whom Jesus heals is that, as the generations pass, it is possible to see ourselves in them. As we look at them, their story becomes our story.

This woman in our scripture lesson has been suffering for 12 years, and more than that, she is sick of her suffering. Mark gives a dig at doctors, " (She) had suffered much under many physicians, and had spent all that she had, and was no better but rather grew worse." (Mark 5:26) This poor woman is sick of being sick.

What was true then is true now. Whenever I go to my hometown, my Grandma looks me square in the eye and says, "Doctors! They just make you sick!" I have little rebuttal since my Grandmother is 104 years old.

There is good reason for Mark's disdain for doctors. When I read the commentaries, there were all sorts of horrible things that doctors prescribed back then. One remedy was to carry the ashes of a burned up ostrich egg. Another cure was to pulverize rubber, alum, and garden crocuses into a goblet of wine and drink it. Another was to carry around a barley seed found in the dung of a flawless female donkey. Imagine dropping that prescription off at CVS. So, of course, she had given up on doctors.

She is suffering; and she is sick to death of her suffering. She is sick of doctors. Her suffering has made her poor. We do not know anything about her, but with 12 years of menstrual bleeding it is likely that she had .trouble conceiving. She may not have had family to help care for her – which was a big deal in those times.

64

And it gets worse. Almost certainly, she is unable to worship God. The temple laws say that if you have any blemish, any disease, any open sores, you are forbidden from worshipping God. During your menses, you are forbidden from the temple. With her 12 years of hemorrhaging, she is barred from worshipping God. And so, she is suffering, bleeding, poor, sick of suffering, and she is cut off from God.

She hears that Jesus is coming through town. She has heard about him. What happens next I think is often misunderstood. She says, "If I touch even his garments, then I shall be made well."

She reaches out. She touches his cloak. She touches not even his skin, not his hand. She touches his cloak. And immediately she is made well. Jesus feels some power come out from him. There is a connection. Something happens.

She trembles, afraid. She has been suffering for so long, seeking answers for so long, and she finally encounters exactly what she needs.

Jesus says, "Daughter your faith has made you well. Go in peace, you are healed of your disease."

So, here's the second point: what about her faith? When Jesus says this, "Daughter your faith has made you well," it makes it sound like she has perfect faith. If only I had faith like that, I would be cured of my disease, my brokenness. If only I had faith like that, I would be healed.

When you look at this exchange closely, what I realize is that her faith was not perfect. In fact, her faith was a little messy. Her faith was even super-stitious. She approached him the way one might approach a wizard ("I know if I touch his cloak, I shall be healed"). Her faith was desperate and messy and bloody. But her faith was also raw and honest – which is all that Jesus needs to work with us.

She had given up on every doctor, every cure, all of society which shunned her. What was special about her faith was not that it was so perfect, but rather it was so raw, so real, so desperate.

She didn't need only healing of her bleeding uterus. She needed healing of her broken heart. She needed complete restoration with God. She needed reconciliation from all the alienation she had suffered from her community. She wanted to feel better.

Maybe even she did not realize it, but when she reached out to Jesus, she did not reach out to Jesus as a means to her salvation, but AS her salvation. Jesus was her salvation.

This story is a comfort to me. We don't need a perfectly worked out, sophisticated faith. We need an honest faith, a raw, "come help me" kind of faith, without pretense, without bargaining.

Of all the people who were pressing in on Jesus, touching his cloak, why her? Maybe everyone else pressing in on Jesus saw Jesus as a means to their own ends, their own version of salvation? Help me with my job. Help me get more money. Help me be a better parent....

Maybe sometimes we approach Jesus the way we approach a doctor. "I am sick, fix me." "I need a pill." "Oh Jesus, help me with my job, my life, my mortgage, my back pain." Maybe, at some deep level, we see Jesus as means to our version of happiness.

Our God who loves us wants something more from us. God wants our heart, raw and open and honest.

The third point: what does Jesus think about her? When all of this business happens with the bleeding woman, Jesus is on his way to rescue Jairus' daughter. Jesus' entourage has just hit the shore. Jairus comes out of the synagogue to great him. Jairus is an important person. For one thing, he has a name. He is a temple leader. Jairus dutifully humbles himself before Jesus – which is an amazing thing unto itself. But then again, Jairus is desperate, worried sick about his daughter. As Jesus hurries to Jairus' home, he stops.

Instead of blowing through the crowds, Jesus heals a socially marginalized, ritually unclean woman, and makes the powerful, male temple leader wait, while his daughter is dying. You can imagine the scene.

Jesus always gives priority to the nameless ones, the suffering, the marginalized, the hurting. The world judges those on the margins so harshly. Jesus always reaches out to the marginalized with such tenderness.

While all this is happening Jairus' daughter dies. There is wailing and commotion. At some level, you could imagine deep resentment towards Jesus, but the story isn't over.

While the healing of the bleeding woman is very public, the healing of Jairus' daughter is very private. Jesus heals not like a physician with pills or potions. Jesus heals with authority, because he is the author. He is the Creator. He is also the Father, and uses the words of intimacy and familiarity, "Talitha cum," "Little girl, arise."

In this moment, we see in Jesus the pure incarnate love of God. Jesus is much more than savior from our sin, much more than moral teacher. Jesus saves lives. The quality of our faith does not earn this salvation. It is love. It is grace. Jesus Christ comes so that the parts of you that are bleeding, hurting, guilty, and hopeless would know true love and true healing. Here is our Jesus who says to us and to all, "Talitha, Talya cum." "Little girl, little boy, arise." Amen.

A Mother's Prayer to a General

At that very time there were some present who told him about the Galileans whose blood Pilate had mingled with their sacrifices. He asked them, "Do you think that because these Galileans suffered in this way they were worse sinners than all other Galileans? No, I tell you; but unless you repent, you will all perish as they did. Or those eighteen who were killed when the tower of Siloam fell on them—do you think that they were worse offenders than all the others living in Jerusalem? No, I tell you; but unless you repent, you will all perish just as they did."

Then he told this parable: "A man had a fig tree planted in his vineyard; and he came looking for fruit on it and found none. So he said to the gardener, 'See here! For three years I have come looking for fruit on this fig tree, and still I find none. Cut it down! Why should it be wasting the soil?' He replied, 'Sir, let it alone for one more year, until I dig around it and put manure on it. If it bears fruit next year, well and good; but if not, you can cut it down.'"

~ LUKE 13:1-9

Loving, Wonderful God, You are our God. We seek you. We thirst for you. Hear our cry, O God, that you would come to us, Living Water. Bless these words, that they may be yours. In Christ's name, Amen.

This is the prayer of a mother whose child is a patient in the pediatric intensive care unit. "O God, you are my God. I seek you. My soul thirsts for you. My flesh faints for you, as in a dry and weary land."

In addition to some daytime clinic duties, as a resident, I have been spending a few over-night shifts in the Pediatric Intensive Care Unit. One day, I showed up to hear about the patients whom I would be caring for that night. When I heard their stories, my heart sank.

One child had an inoperable tumor. But then had suffered complications and needed urgent surgery to have half of his intestines taken out.

Another child was recovering from brain surgery. She had been playing with her dolls the day before. Now, she was paralyzed on the right side of her body.

Another little girl had come in with end-stage HIV. Another baby, just a baby, had a congenital heart defect and needed urgent surgery.

I stood in the middle of this room with these kids in their beds and their frightening, heart breaking stories. I saw the moms and dads with their faces chiseled with pain and worry.

"O God, you are my God. I seek you. My soul thirsts for you. My flesh faints for you, as in a dry and weary land." This is the prayer that I imagine for those kids and those worried, scared moms and dads. "O God, you are my God. I seek you. My soul thirsts for you. My flesh faints for you, as in a dry and weary land."

This is the psalm we sang this morning. This is the prayer of the suffering heart. When there is nothing left to cling to but the God of Hope.

These words, "O God, you are my God. I seek you. My soul thirsts for you." These words are almost 3,000 years old, but these words give shape to the pain. These words articulate so well the great pain and loneliness and depths that afflict all our lives.

The depths can get very deep indeed. Not every kid makes it out of the Pediatric Intensive Care Unit. All of us, in our lives, will suffer. This prayer - "O God you are my God" - is OUR prayer.

I want to talk about two things. First, I want to talk about when other people suffer. And I want to talk about when you suffer.

First, when other people suffer. When other people suffer, inside our heads, we make a judgment, don't we? Unless you are on the list to be canonized by the Pope, somewhere in your brain, you make a judgment. Did they deserve their suffering or not?

Floyd wrapped his car around a tree. Ah, but he was drinking wasn't he? Ah, yes, we think to ourselves, he deserved it.

Tina got mugged on Blatchley Avenue. Ah, but she should not have been walking around the streets alone at night.

Sometimes, there is even no direct, causal relationship, but we still make a judgment. . . . Ziggy got fired from his job . . . . But he deserved it, because I didn't like him much anyway.

This is exactly what Jesus was talking about in the temple. "Those 18 people who died when the tower in Siloam fell on them. You thought they were sinners? That they deserved it? Well, you are just as big a sinner as those guys were."

"When Pontius Pilate killed those people in the temple while they were making sacrifices, do think they were worse sinners than you?"

"Unless you repent," Jesus says, "You will all perish just as they did."

Jesus is not being very pastoral, very nurturing, in this passage. This is not his, "I-am-the-good-shepherd-you-are-the-light-of-the-world" speech.

This is the question behind what he is saying: Do you want what you deserve? Do you want to be treated objectively? Tally up the balance of our lives, and have God hand us what we have earned, what you have earned. How much does it take to *earn* eternity? How good does one have to be to merit God's favor?

There was a fig tree. It would not bear fruit. The owner was going to cut it down. Cut it down! For three years there has been no fruit. It is taking up soil! But then, Jesus says, there is the Gardener who will nourish it, tender it, nurture it. Maybe then, the fig tree will bear fruit.

"Unless you repent," Jesus says, "you will all perish just as they did."

So judge not *their* hearts, but rather turn *your* own heart to God. The Gardener who is our Christ will nourish us, tender us, nurture us, and yes, die for us. We do not get what we deserve. We get Christ. We do not get judged the way we ought to be. Christ gets judged the way we ought. So, when the tower of Siloam falls on our neighbor, let us not judge them, but rather let us be to them the Gardener that nurtures them, as Christ nurtures us.

Now what about when we suffer. We know suffering. "O God, you are my God. I seek you. My soul thirsts for you. My flesh faints for you, as in a dry and weary land."

I came across the wise words from a theologian and writer named Nikos Kazantzakis. He is Greek and wrote the book Zorba the Greek, which was a huge movie many years ago. This is what he writes about prayer and suffering.

"My prayer is not the whimpering of a beggar nor a confession of love. Nor is my prayer the trivial reckoning of a tradesman: Give me and I shall give you. My prayer is the report of a soldier to his General: This is what I did today, this is how I fought to save the entire battle in my own sector, these are the obstacles I found, this is how I plan to fight tomorrow. My God and I are horsemen galloping in the burning sun or under the drizzling rain. Pale, starving, but unsubdued, we ride and converse.

"Leader!" I cry. He turns his face towards me, and I shudder to confront his anguish.

Our love for each other is rough and ready, we sit at the same table, we drink the same wine in this low tavern of life."*

There are many images for God. There is the tender Good Shepherd, God the Almighty Father, the Great Physician, the Light of the World, Wisdom, the Spirit, the Counselor, the God of the Burning Bush, the God who blew on the great emptiness to make the heavens and earth. God is very big.

I like this image - God the General. God and I, we ride together. Sometimes the desert is hot. Sometimes the rain drenches me. Sometimes I have found the favor of the world. Sometimes, I am despised by the world. But God and I, we ride, we ride. I try to keep up. I ride as hard as can, live the best life I can.

At the end of the day, I pray, "O God, you are my God. I seek you. My soul thirsts for you. My flesh faints for you, as in a dry and weary land." (Psalm 63:1)

At the end of the day, my God and General gives me shelter in that tavern. My God, my General, gives me drink, so that I may thirst no more.

---

* Kazantzakis, Nikos. *Saviors of God*. Simon and Schuster, 2012, page 103.

"My prayer is not the whimpering of a beggar nor a confession of love. Nor is my prayer the trivial reckoning of a tradesman: Give me and I shall give you.

My prayer is the report of a soldier to his General: This is what I did today, this is how I fought to save the entire battle in my own sector, these are the obstacles I found, this is how I plan to fight tomorrow."*

"O God, you are my God. I seek you. My soul thirsts for you. My flesh faints for you, as in a dry and weary land." (Psalm 63:1) That is the cry of a soldier of the faith - King David - seeking his General.

The Psalm continues, "You have been my help. In the shadow of your wings, I sing for joy. My soul clings to you; your right hand upholds me." This prayer of suffering is also the prayer of faith.

As if in response, from a passage even older than this psalm come the words of Isaiah, "Ho, everyone who thirsts, come to the waters; and you that have no money, come, buy and eat! (Isaiah 55:1)

O God, you are my God. I seek you. "My soul thirsts for you. My flesh faints for you, as in a dry and weary land." (Psalm 63:1)

"Ho, everyone who thirsts, come to the waters; and you that have no money, come, buy and eat!" (Isaiah 55:1)

Our God who is our General guides us, protects us, and nourishes us, so that we thirst no more, so that we are no longer faith. So that we can ride with our General and our God, soldiers of the faith. This is the good news. This is the power of the Gospel. Amen.

The Time of Death

When the hour came, he took his place at the table, and the apostles with him. He said to them, "I have eagerly desired to eat this Passover with you before I suffer; for I tell you, I will not eat it until it is fulfilled in the kingdom of God." Then he took a cup, and after giving thanks he said, "Take this and divide it among yourselves; for I tell you that from now on I will not drink of the fruit of the vine until the kingdom of God comes." Then he took a loaf of bread, and when he had given thanks, he broke it and gave it to them, saying, "This is my body, which is given for you. Do this in remembrance of me." And he did the same with the cup after supper, saying, "This cup that is poured out for you is the new covenant in my blood.

~ LUKE *22:1-27*

Loving God, Wonderful God, you enter into our lives, astride a donkey into Jerusalem, amidst our hymns and prayers, and amidst the words you have given us. Bless these words, God, that they would strengthen us in the faith. In Christ's name, Amen.

I want to talk with you about death. In particular, I want to talk about the instant of death, the instant when we die. And then I want to talk about Jesus' death and Palm Sunday, and then a few words about you and me.

I want to share a few personal stories about death. I try not to do that, because the pulpit should not be so much about the experiences of your pastor rather than the word of God. But a few incidents in the past few weeks has affected me deeply, and they bear directly upon our scripture and what we are about on this special day, and so I share them. They are about my patients, for whom I care very deeply. I am protecting their identities, and I am reasonably sure you have not encountered these folks in your life. And so I wish to share with you two stories about death.

The first story about death. I am working in the Emergency Room, and a patch comes in from the paramedics…. Woman, renal failure, found down at home…. No pulse. No respirations. The paramedics push air into her lungs with a ventilation bag. They push on her chest, to keep blood squishing through her body.

When she arrives a minute later in the ER, she is cold. Her eyes have glazed over. There is a hollow silence in her chest. No heartbeat.

And so we begin. The nurses with whom I work are the best I have ever seen. They have seen this hundreds of times. And I, a bit early in my career, several dozen. This poor woman is dead. Suddenly. Dead. One moment alive. The next dead.

And so we begin…. I intubate her. We begin chest compressions. An ampule of adrenaline. A few rounds of bicarb. Several vials of atropine. Nothing. "She won't make it."

More adrenaline. Some mag, a few amps of calcium. More chest compressions…. And then a flitter, a bleb on the monitor. We slap electrodes on her chest. Crank up the amps.

There is a pulse, a few moments, a shudder, and a flicker. "Maybe she will make it, but probably not." And then gone.

More chest compressions. Ventilation. In and out her pulse goes. More epi. More atropine. No pulse…. And then her heart awakens…. Only to fade out again. The line between life and death is hard to define, but this poor woman seems to crawl just on the line. Parts of her have died. Parts are alive. And so we work on.

And then, there is a pulse, weak, thready, slow, but a pulse. We crank up the pacer wires. They capture her heartbeat. There is a slow realization among our team. This woman is not dead. This woman is alive. This woman lives!

When I meet her husband, I find him strangely calm. He says, "Just this morning, my wife said to me that today she was going to die.... She just felt it in her heart. No pains or anything.... She just had this feeling."

And then 12 hours later, she did die, but only for a moment. Now she is alive. Holding on to the line. But in that ER, at that time, alive. She died and then was alive again. I learn that 3 days later, she entered into another similar episode in the Intensive Care Unit from which she did not recover.

Another patient experiences a death of a different kind. She was in the hospital. She came in with incredibly high, bone-crushing fevers and sweats. She has given her life over to crack cocaine and alcohol. I learn that she is infected with HIV and has never taken any medication for it.

She enters the hospital. Turns out she has a tough infection in her bone marrow related to Tuberculosis. With three different antibiotics, she will not die from this infection.

We get to know each other, and then I ask, "You know, that this HIV can kill you... The medications are so good, so powerful, that if you take them, you may live for a long, long time."

"I know that," she tells me.

"Would you like to take the HIV medications."

"Not particularly."

"Why not?" I ask.

"Because I drink too much and that is more important to me."

And so there she sits, the pipe and the bottle, more important than her life. She still has a pulse. She still has a blood pressure. But is she truly alive?

The first patient: when did she die? Did she die in the Emergency Room, or days later in the ER? Did she leave her life behind? Did she die when she had a premonition, a sense that her death was near? She left her life behind – she died – as it were.

Now, the person who wrestles with drugs and alcohol and HIV. She still has a pulse and a blood pressure, but has she left her life behind her? Has she already died.

Death is all around us…. Madrid… Iraq…. Our city streets.

Jesus Christ knew that he was going to die. He enters Jerusalem with a celebration and a parade. And then a few days later, he calls his dearest disciples together for the Passover meal. He tells them, "This is the last time that we shall share wine together until my Father's kingdom fully comes."

Jesus knew he was going to die. He knew he was going to suffer. He knew that it would not be easy. But he also knew, with every confidence, with sure and certain hope, that he would live again.

He tells his disciples, "For which is the greater, one who sits at the table, or the one who serves? Is it not the one who sits at the table. But I am among you as one who serves."

"This is my body broken for you." "This cup which is poured out for you is the new covenant in my blood."

And so when do you die? You are alive in a different way.

Jesus Christ knew he was going to die. And he knew that he was going to live.

Brothers and Sisters, know that your life in him is your life forever.

Who Cares About the Cross When Everything Is Going To Hell?

For God so loved the world that he gave his only Son, so that everyone who believes in him may not perish but may have eternal life.

"Indeed, God did not send the Son into the world to condemn the world, but in order that the world might be saved through him. Those who believe in him are not condemned; but those who do not believe are condemned already, because they have not believed in the name of the only Son of God. And this is the judgment, that the light has come into the world, and people loved darkness rather than light because their deeds were evil. For all who do evil hate the light and do not come to the light, so that their deeds may not be exposed. But those who do what is true come to the light, so that it may be clearly seen that their deeds have been done in God.

~ JOHN 3:14-21

God, you loved the world so much that you sent your Son as helper and savior. Let your Spirit move in these words and in our hearts that you would reach us in the way that we need, that our hearts would grow in the faith. Let your Spirit move, in your Son's name, Amen.

The title of the sermon is meant to be enigmatic, "WHO CARES ABOUT THE CROSS WHEN EVERYTHING IS GOING TO HELL?"

The answer seems obvious at first glance: nobody. "Pastor Ben, my retirement account has been torpedoed and I might not have a job when I show up to work on Monday. Our government is 2 trillion dollars in debt. My own credit card bill is about that much. Our country has lost 5 million jobs. We fight a war in Iraq and Afghanistan. There is no end in sight.... The cross is an abstraction, an empty concept that has no bearing on my life."

I hear this, and I get it. Makes perfect sense to me. Somewhere in the New York Times this past week, a business leader said, "A crises is a terrible thing to waste." Amidst all that is going on, I interpret this to mean that now is the time to question our beliefs, to examine what matters to us the most. What seemed certain – our future, our jobs, everything – is now uncertain.

I want to talk about faith and belief. In particular, as we get closer to Easter, I want to talk about our belief in the cross. There is the line from the gospel of John, "The Son of Man must be lifted up that whoever believes in him will have eternal life." (John 3:14-15)

I think the cross can be a stumbling block for our faith. Churches tend to minimize the cross or maximize the cross. Here is what I mean: some churches emphasize that Jesus was a great teacher, the Son of God, who loved everyone, and healed everyone, but when it comes to the bloody business of dying for our sins, some churches gloss over this part of scripture. We skip Golgotha as it were and go right to the Easter lilies. The downside to this approach is that it minimizes who Jesus was. Sure, Jesus was a good teacher and all, but he was more than that wasn't he?

Then there are the churches that maximize the cross. We are all sinners. We are going to hell. Jesus paid the debt that we could not pay. "Jesus died for our sins." We say that all the time in church, but what does this really mean? The best metaphor to understand Christ on the cross goes like this: Jesus on the cross is like a cosmic government bailout for our debaucherous lifestyle of credit-default-swaps and mortgage-backed securities.

This belief in the cross gets at the fact that we human beings have an amazing ability to really mess ourselves up; and something a lot bigger than ourselves is needed to make it right again. And yet, the language of "sacrifice" and "dying on the cross for our sins" is shocking to our modern sensibilities.

To ancient civilizations, this idea of a sacrifice to pay off their sins was completely within their understanding. People sacrificed at the temple all the time – a turtle dove for this broken law, a lamb for another broken law. Every religion in the Middle East at the time demanded blood sacrifices. The Greeks, the Romans, the Syrians, and the Egyptians – they all had a very sophisticated payback model. At its core, it makes sense. You do something wrong, you pay the price. As it was in the marketplace, so it is in your relationship with God.

What was incredibly liberating for the early Christians is that Jesus Christ, the Lamb of God, could pay off your debts once and for all. No more blood sacrifices in the temple. Jesus *was* the sacrifice. This was a revolutionary, outrageous claim that unsettled every belief system of its time.

And yet, here we are, a long way from the temple in Jerusalem, and soon to face the Easter cross. What do we make of this Jesus suffering on the cross for our sins?

I want to wrestle with this question by looking carefully at this passage in the Gospel of John. This passage is an exchange between Jesus and a Pharisee, a temple leader, named Nicodemus. Nicodemus is the stand-in for the modern person. He is sophisticated, successful, educated, and politically savvy. But, something is not quite right with his life, and so late at night, when no one else is around, he seeks an encounter with Jesus. Nicodemus is the modern person.

Nicodemus is the guy with the cell phone, the blackberry, and three computers who hasn't had a real conversation in 6 months.

Nicodemus is the single mom of three kids, trying to keep it together, wondering what the purpose of it all is.

Nicodemus is the elderly woman so painfully lonely, who sits alone, uncertain what the future will hold.

Nicodemus is the guy who played by the rules all his life, but just got laid off. What does it all mean? I look at Nicodemus, and I see you, me, and everyone.

One of my favorite physicians is an oncologist Rachel Remen, who said about the crisis recently, "You see the star most brightly after it has grown dark. The problem is that it *has* grown dark and people realize that they have not been living by *any* star."*

And so, you, me, Nicodemus come to Jesus in the dark of night seeking a star. We come with a question, "Jesus, are you for real?" Every person in this church asks this question, "Jesus, are you for real?" "Do you matter for my life?" "Do I matter for your life?"

What I believe to be the answer to this question, I will say in two different ways – a Biblical way and a modern way. First, the Biblical way from a loose translation called The Message: "This is how much God loved the world: He gave his Son, his one and only Son. And this is why: so that no one need be destroyed; by believing in him, anyone can have a whole and lasting life. God didn't go to all the trouble of sending his Son merely to point an accusing finger, telling the world how bad it was. He came to help, to put the world right again." (John 3:16-17)

Here is a modern way of understanding this passage: God does not seek value, God creates value. You are valued because you are loved. This love is a gift, not an achievement.

---

* Speaking of Faith, National Public Radio, March 5th, 2009, accessed on line www.npr.org, March 6th, 2009.

This is where we modern people get hung up, because in every other part of our lives, we are judged by the world. You get good grades at school or bad grades. You are picked for the softball team, or not. You are a "cool kid" or not. You are hired. You are fired. You are measured, rated, stacked one against another.

Through it all, you have to sacrifice. You do not sacrifice a lamb, or a dove, but you sacrifice blood nonetheless. You sacrifice your blood, and it is never enough. And the next day, you sacrifice more and more. It is never enough, because the world never stops judging you. The world demands a blood sacrifice.

But all God wants is to love you. Because of this love, you are valued. It is not the other way around – you are valuable so you are loved – for this is the way the world works. Instead, you are loved by God, and so you are valued. And so, you do not need to bleed yourselves anymore to find value in your life.

There was a wonderful theologian named Jaroslav Pelikan who died a few years back. He wrote a book called, Credo, in which he collected statements of faith from different Christian denominations around the world. I discovered that one of his favorites came from the Congregation of the Holy Ghost – the church of the Masai people of Eastern Nigeria. I caught him speaking on NPR's show Speaking of Faith. They took the ancient beliefs of the church and enlivened it with their own language. This is their statement of faith:

> "We believe in one high God, who out of love created the beautiful world. We believe that God made good His promise by sending His Son, Jesus Christ, a man in the flesh, a Jew by tribe, born poor in a little village, who left His home and was always on safari doing good, curing people by the power of God, teaching about God and man, and showing that the meaning of religion is love. He was rejected by His people, tortured and nailed hands and feet to a

cross, and died. He was buried in the grave, but the hyenas did not touch Him, and on the third day He rose from the grave."*

I am grateful for this perspective of Jesus, because I see him with new eyes. This creed connects the ministry of Jesus with the resurrection of Jesus. When you take away the traditions, the stained glass, the cathedrals, the liturgy, what you have is the Son of God always on a safari, doing good, teaching that the meaning of religion is love. When he dies, even the hyenas do not touch him. The evil of the world does not hold him back. On the third day, he rises from the grave.

I believe that the cross is a tragedy, because the world demands blood. Love, before it is understood, will always be rejected. If Jesus had changed every heart, if Jesus had restored Eden, there would have been no one to nail him to a cross. The world would have known the love of God. Instead, the world demands a sacrifice. Evil is strong.

The cross is a tragedy, but at the same time, the cross is a victory, because the powers of the world are not nearly as strong as the love of God. The hyenas do not touch our Jesus, and the hatred of the world does not hold him back. On the third day he rises from the grave. You do not need to sacrifice your blood to be loved by God. God sends his Son into the world, that whoever places their trust in him, whoever believes in his safari, that person shall not perish, but shall know a whole life, a life eternal in His name. This is the good news, Amen.

---

* Tippet, K. (Host). (2009 October 23rd) The Need for Creeds, guest Jaroslav Pelikan, [Radio Broadcast Episode] *Speaking of Faith*. Washington, DC: National Public Radio, accessed online October 23rd, 2009.

The Mustard Seed in the Ashe of Suffering

Judah has gone into exile with suffering
and hard servitude;
she lives now among the nations,
and finds no resting place;
her pursuers have all overtaken her
in the midst of her distress.

~ *LAMENTATIONS 1:3*

The apostles said to the Lord, "Increase our faith!" The
Lord replied, "If you had faith the size of a mustard seed,
you could say to this mulberry tree, 'Be uprooted and
planted in the sea,' and it would obey you.

~ *LUKE 17:5-10*

Loving, Wonderful, Holy God, in our lamentations, our cries of suffering, you come to us. Come to us now, by your Spirit, in these words and our meditations, to strengthen us in the faith. In Christ's name, Amen.

This is the fundamental question of our faith: what do you do in face of suffering? When we face the death of a spouse, a frightening diagnosis, the loss of a job, and on and on, what does our heart do? How do we handle this?

In the face of suffering, some come to God for comfort, from an inexplicable need, deep from the heart, to find a space of peace and rest from it all.

In the face of suffering, others may raise an angry fist at God, curse God, fling accusations, and flee God scowling into a place of spiritual desolation.

To help us address this, I want to share three stories: the first is a story about the suffering of a nation, the second a story of a friend of mine, the third, a story about the disciples which includes the disciples back then and you and me right now.

First, the suffering of a nation. Old Jeremiah had been shooting his mouth of for years. The people scoffed. Isaiah too let it rip with prophecy and warnings. But the nation did not listen. Then mad man Ezekiel, from up north, with his tongue of fire, spelled disaster. No one listened.

And finally, in the year 586 before the birth of the Savior, it happened. The Babylonians roared across the desert. A hoard seething with strength and fierce anger. The most powerful nation on earth took on a small kingdom, a nation that had once been slaves in Egypt. The Babylonians crushed the Hebrews. Jerusalem burned. The temple, the beloved temple that the prophets so lovingly described down to the last stone, crumbled to the ground. The home of their faith, the sanctum sanctorum, the dwelling place of God, was destroyed. God had no more home on earth. In the course of a day, the Hebrew nation was destroyed. It was their 9-11, Pearl Harbor Day, and Hiroshima all at once.

The poor and ill were left to die. The talented and rich were carted off to Babylon to serve as slaves. In the ash and rubble of their suffering, a prophet cried out, "How lonely sits the city that once was full of people! How like a widow she has become, she that was great among the nations! She that was a princess among the provinces has become a vassal. She weeps bitterly in the night, with tears on her cheeks; among all her lovers she has no one to comfort her; her friend have dealt treacherously with her, they have become her enemies."

The story of the Old Testament, the Hebrew Bible, is about 1000 pages long and it spans around 4000 years of history. It can be broken down into four movements. Homecoming – when the Hebrews found their land of milk and honey. Building their family – the story of the great kings such as David and Solomon. Destruction – the fall of Jerusalem. And then, as if to complete a holy circle, homecoming again. From the ash and rubble of their suffering, their nation was reborn. The city was rebuilt. The people returned. Even their joy returned, but it was a joy that was tempered with memory. There was deep gratitude in their homecoming, for the memory of their loss deepened their joy, made it more seasoned, more mature.

"The roads to Zion mourn; all her gates are desolate, her priests groan; her young girls grieve, an her lot is bitter." But from those broken stones, amidst this broken and suffering world, they rebuilt their city. And God restored their hope and their joy.

The second story is about a friend of mine. I call him Coach. I came to the ER to do an overnight shift. And there was Coach, a seasoned, experienced, caring ER doctor, a devoted family man, a veteran of little leagues over the years (hence his affection nickname). And there he was in the ER at 11:30 at night. Normally, this is not unusual, but in this case, he was not scheduled to work. He was not dressed in hospital gear. He had a tear in his eye.

"Coach, what brings you here?"
"My father just died."

The gang gathered around and heard the story. About the long illness, about the ventilator, about the agonizing decision to pull away the drips, about how the blood pressure was too low to continue dialysis, about the seizures his father suffered. And finally, about the vigil at the bedside, the family gathered around, waiting for his father's death.

And it came, every heartbeat monitored: 60 beats a minute, then 50, then 30, for a long time 30 beats a minute, and then 20, and then only a few, and then, it was finished. The long ordeal, the suffering, finished.

I am fascinated about the faith and spiritual perspectives of my physician and nurse colleagues. They are a smart bunch, trained in a strong intellectual tradition, death and suffering are their daily companions. And I consider myself a good friend to this man I fondly call "Coach."

He said to me at that midnight hour amidst the rumble and loneliness of an Emergency Room, "My faith became real in all this. I found myself praying. Not so much for miracles, but for peace, for God's will to be done. And I felt God there at the bedside. I felt Him. I knew my father was in a good place, and that he had found his rest."

"The roads to Zion mourn; all her gates are desolate, her priests groan; her young girls grieve, and her lot is bitter." But from those broken stones, amidst this broken and suffering world, the Hebrews rebuilt their city. God restored their hope and their joy. At the bedside of his dying father, God comforted my friend and my coach.

Third, I want to talk about Jesus' disciples. About them of years ago, and about you and me and the mission of our church. The disciples cried out, "Increase our faith." And Jesus launches into a story, where he says in essence, "The servants of God do what they are called to do. That is their call, their mission, their duty. If you had the faith of the smallest of seeds – a mustard seed – you could move mountains."

If you have ever stood in the ash and rubble of suffering, you have stood with the people of God. We live in a rough world. Planes fall out of the sky. The rubble of our suffering has pushed us to war. We live in a fallen world. Yet, amidst the rubble, God has given us a taste of heaven at the communion table and the fellowship of this church. While the kingdom of God may alight in our heart, it has not fully come. "I am the alpha and the omega. The beginning and the end." And the end will come. And we shall know our God face to face.

And so here we are, the disciples of God. Inheritors of this great lineage of homecoming, building, and rebuilding. Our city. Our church. Our heart.

God raises up the stones so Zion may be whole again. God raises up His Son that we might live again. God raises you from the ash and rubble of your suffering, that we might be the disciples of God, shepherds of joy. This is the promise of God, Amen.

Thinking

Must you leave your brain at the door before entering church?

Does not wisdom call,
and does not understanding raise her voice?
On the heights, beside the way,
at the crossroads she takes her stand;
beside the gates in front of the town,
at the entrance of the portals she cries out:
"To you, O people, I call,
and my cry is to all that live.

~ PROVERBS *8:1-4*

Loving God, we pray that the Spirit of truth, and come in this moment, in our meditations, in these words. We pray that your Spirit of truth will come, that you would strengthen our faith, and that we might find our joy and our true home with you. In Christ's name, Amen

"When the Lord established the heavens, I was there, … when he marked out the foundations of the earth, then I was beside him, like a master worker; and I was daily his delight, rejoicing before him always, rejoicing in his inhabited world and delighting in the human race." (Proverbs 8:27-31) The "I" in this paragraph is Wisdom. Proverbs personifies Wisdom, makes Wisdom to be a person. Many Biblical scholars write that Wisdom-as-person is a literary device so that we can better understand how God created the universe. Wisdom is part of the created order of the universe. Wisdom is a master-worker. Wisdom is the delight of God.

In our modern life together, we don't think so much about Wisdom as we do about Logic. We are a reasonable, logical people. We want proof. We want facts. Maybe Wisdom has fallen out of our modern parlance.

In that spirit, I would like to read to you a dialogue between Wisdom and Logic to illustrate a point. This dialogue actually happened, more or less. It is a conversation between President Nelson Mandela of South Africa, his top advisor, and the South African Rugby Federation. This conversation came from the movie Invictus which is a movie about the first months of Nelson Mandela's presidency in South Africa. The movie uses the Springboks national rugby team as emblematic of the tensions in post-apartheid South Africa. The Springboks team, with their white players, their green and gold jerseys, was just one more symbol of white rule and apartheid. Rugby, a European, "white" sport.

In the great tide of support for President Mandela and the overthrow of apartheid, the South African Rugby league votes to disband the Springboks rugby team, the national rugby team of South Africa. They vote to change the name, to get rid of the colors, to fire the players.

When President Mandela hears that the Rugby Board votes to disband the Springboks rugby team, he leaves the Japanese Trade delegation, he drops what he is doing and speeds off to the Rugby board meeting.

For the purpose of this illustration, President Mandela, played by Morgan Freeman, is Wisdom. His top advisor is Logic. Here is how it goes.

As he speeds off to intervene in this meeting, Logic says, "You risk alienating your people, your cabinet, your party."

"Your advice is duly noted," says Wisdom.

Logic: "The people want this. They hate the Springboks. They do not want to be represented by a team they cheered against all their lives."

Wisdom: "In this instance, the people are wrong, and as their elected leader, it is my job to show them that."

Logic: "Your are risking your political capital. You are risking your future as our leader."

Wisdom: "The day I am afraid to do that is the day I am no longer fit to lead."

Logic: "At least risk your political capital for something more important than rugby."

The President barnstorms into the crowded meeting and says, "Brothers, Sisters, Comrades. I am here because I believe that you have made a decision with insufficient information and foresight. I am aware of your earlier vote. I am aware that it was unanimous. Nonetheless I believe we should restore the Springboks, restore their name, their emblem, and their colors. Immediately. Let me tell you why. On Robben Island, in prison, all of my jailers were Afrikaners. For 27 years I studied them. I learned their language, read their books, their poetry. I had to know my enemy before I could prevail against them. And we did prevail. Did we not? All of us here. We prevailed. Our enemy is no longer the Afrikaners. They are our fellow South Africans, our partners in democracy. And they treasure Springboks rugby. If we take that away we lose them. We prove we are what they feared we would be. We have to be better than that. We have to surprise them with compassion and restraint and generosity. I know, we must surprise them with all the things they denied us. But this is no time to celebrate petty revenge. The is the time to build our nation with using every single brick available to us… even if the brick is wrapped in green and gold. If we take away what they cherish, the Springboks, we reinforce the cycle of fear between us. I will do what I must to stop that cycle or it will destroy us."

This speech sways the Rugby Board to re-instate the Springboks by one vote. As the movie unfolds, the Springboks rugby team reaches out to the black townships. As the world cup gathers steam, all South Africans, black and white, rally around the Springboks rugby team. Of course, today, the Springboks team is completely integrated. The work of wisdom.

Now Logic demands proof, evidence, a sound argument. Logic weighs in the balance all the competing interests. Now the National Rugby Federation had every reason to claim power for themselves, restore justice. President Mandela's advisor had every reason, even responsibility, to present a cogent argument against his outrageous behavior. Go along with the majority. Do not waste your political capital. Exact revenge. Banish the Springboks rugby team as a vile symbol of apartheid. I find this amazing. It all makes perfect sense. Logic is correct.

But Wisdom sees beyond logic. I should pause here to define Wisdom. I poked around a little bit to get a working definition. In the book of Proverbs, in the original Hebrew, there are a few words that define Wisdom. Basically, Wisdom means, "to notice little distinctions in things," or, "to know how things really work." There is a famous theologian named Gerhard VanRaad who defined Wisdom as "Being competent in the regards to the reality of life."

Why am I talking about all of this? We live in a society that loves logic and reason and information. The problem is that for most things in our lives, there is not enough evidence. There is no perfect rule to guide us. Yes, every religion has rules, and I am not saying they are wrong, but life is more complicated than that.

Who do you marry? What should your career be? Should I change jobs? Should I confront that person? Should I hold back? Should I move out of my house? Should I move in with my parents? Should my parents move in with me? How do I know that God exists?

There are no hard and fast rules for any of those decisions. Knowledge and Logic is not enough. Wisdom is when we do the right thing when there are no rules that apply.

Some people live by rules, logic, and reason. In the same way, other people make decisions with their heart, their instinct. Things have to *feel* right. "I walked into that apartment, and I felt déjà vu." "I just know in my heart of hearts, this is the right person to marry." "I feel the presence of God."

There is the mind. The mind demands proof, facts and logic. "Prove me to me existence of God." There is the heart that has feeling and instinct. There is the space in between. The mind wants proof. "Prove to me the existence of God." The heart goes with instinct and feeling. If it feels true, it probably is true. But wisdom is different. Wisdom is both purely reasonable and purely of the heart.

Maybe we do not think about Wisdom, because we think of it as one of those religious stuffy words. In Proverbs, wisdom takes on the persona of a person. It's a literary device, a poetic manipulation. Wisdom as a person. But, what if the wisdom of God *really was a person*. What if you did not get wisdom from a set of rules in a book, but wisdom came to you in a person. With all the hard stuff of life, wrestling with illness, job changes, what to do with finances and family and love, all the big struggles of life, what if we had a relationship with a person who could help us? What if we had a relationship with someone who really was the wisdom of God?

And the prophet Isaiah cries out, "He will be called Wonderful Counselor, Mighty God, Everlasting Father, Prince of Peace. Of the increase of his government and peace there will be no end. (Is 9:6-7)

The Proverbs are about Jesus. I re-read our morning lesson, "When the Lord established the heavens, (Jesus) was there, ... when (the Lord) marked out the foundations of the earth, then (Jesus) was beside him, like a master worker; and (Jesus) was daily his delight, rejoicing before him always, rejoicing in his inhabited world and delighting in the human race." (Proverbs 8:27-31)

Jesus. The wisdom of God. Rejoicing. Delighting. The foundation of the earth. Who guides us, who helps us, who saves us. This is the good news. Thanks be to God. Amen.

Can a Christian Decide Against a G-Tube?

But Thomas (who was called the Twin), one of the twelve, was not with them when Jesus came. So the other disciples told him, "We have seen the Lord." But he said to them, "Unless I see the mark of the nails in his hands, and put my finger in the mark of the nails and my hand in his side, I will not believe." A week later his disciples were again in the house, and Thomas was with them. Although the doors were shut, Jesus came and stood among them and said, "Peace be with you." Then he said to Thomas, "Put your finger here and see my hands. Reach out your hand and put it in my side. Do not doubt but believe." Thomas answered him, "My Lord and my God!" Jesus said to him, "Have you believed because you have seen me? Blessed are those who have not seen and yet have come to believe." Now Jesus did many other signs in the presence of his disciples, which are not written in this book. But these are written so that you may come to believe that Jesus is the Messiah, the Son of God, and that through believing you may have life in his name.

~ JOHN *20:24-31*

Loving, Holy God, your Son is risen, victorious over death. And yet still we come with our doubts and our hang-ups. Use these words. Use Your Word. Use Your Spirit, that you could move in our hearts and reaffirm for us your love in our lives. In Christ's name, Amen.

A lot has happened in the past few days. There have been two notable deaths: Terri Shaivo and Pope John Paul. Their leave-taking from this world during the season of Easter has incited in me reflection about our lives and our purpose in the world.

I would like to wrestle with a fundamental question. Can a Christian decline a G-tube? A G-tube is short for gastrostomy tube or gastric tube. It is a plastic tube that goes from the skin of the abdomen directly into the stomach so that a person can receive nutrition if they cannot eat for themselves. It measures about 2 inches. It is not high-tech. The diet is usually a special adult nutrition drink. This question takes many forms. If a Christian is presented with a choice - take food the rest of your life and live in a vegetative state or decline the artificial feeds and let nature take its course – what does the Christian choose?

I speak to this issue because you may one day be in the position to decide this question for yourself, for a loved one. What you believe in the core of your being, your heart of hearts, will reflect what you do in a very direct way. One day, we may all end up in a position requiring a feeding tube, and it is better to have these conversations in a thoughtful way before the situation arises.

It would seem that the Christian should choose, must choose, the artificial feeds. The story of Terri Shaivo is tragic and heart-wrenching. There was also a bilious, nasty public side: a debate between the husband who seemed to move on and the parents clinging beyond all hope. Add a veneer of political posturing, image of Jesse Jackson praying with the family, President Bush weighing in from the White House, and the answer seems obvious: keep the feeds going, keep Terri Shaivo alive at all costs. I do not want to dissect the medical aspects of Mrs. Shaivo's story but I do want to think about the spiritual and ethical implications of what happened.

Now the first lesson that Terri Shaivo teaches us all is to have a living will. Usually this is a document prepared in concert a lawyer, but simply expressing your wishes on paper, or even expressing your wishes to your next of kin actually suffices. In my role as a doctor, all the time, family members share with me the wishes of their loved one. "Do everything Doc, she would want everything." "She would not want to suffer anymore than she already has…. Let nature take its course."

And so, as your pastor, on a pragmatic level, I ask this of everyone: get a living will. Or, at the very least, write down what you would want should you become incapacitated, or talk to your closest family members about what your wishes would be. You are doing yourselves a favor, and your family. Families are often put in the uncomfortable position of not knowing what their parents would want. And so, let us know. Would you want a G-tube to keep you alive if you were in a vegetative state?

Based on the opinions of Jesse Jackson, George Bush, the United States Congress, and just about every other God-fearing American who appreciates the sanctity of human life, the obvious choice is to choose the G-tube. Keep me alive. At all costs. At all times.

I may be unpopular. I may be in the minority. But I want us all to just consider three reasons why a Christian may decide against a feeding tube. I am not saying MUST decide against a feeding tube, but rather MAY decide against a feeding tube.

First, we are people of the resurrection. "Nothing will ever separate us from the love of God," neither powers, nor principalities, life nor death. We are Easter people, children of God. Our Lord is a man who rose from the dead who tells us that in our living, we live in Him. In our dying, we die in Him. And one day, in a blink of an eye, with the sound of the angels' trumpet, we shall rise again.

The passage we read today about the "Doubting Thomas" points to this deep question about resurrection: just what was Jesus talking about anyway? A resurrection of the soul, a "We-will-carry-his-memory-with-us-forever" sort of eternal life. Or did Jesus mean real resurrection in the body, eternal life in the body? We all have had doubting Thomas inside of us. Thomas had to put his hands in Christ's wounds before he could believe; he was that incredulous. We are followers of a risen Christ. Death is not the end for us. We are people of the resurrection, a real resurrection.

Second, we are people of life, real life. The life that God intends for us is a true, whole, vibrant life. If you are blind, Christ heals you. If you have a lame arm, Christ straightens it. If you are paralyzed, Christ gives you strength. If you are afflicted with demons, Christ casts them out. The life God intends for us is a real one, made whole and strong.

Disease is part of the brokenness of this world, and one day, our bodies will be whole and strong again. God will bring us back to Eden, back to his House of many rooms. I wonder if keeping my pulse going and my respirations going although my mind has left me is in keeping with God's plan. Just because medical science can keep me alive, should I be kept alive if my life is not the life that God intends for me? In the same way we play God by putting criminals to death, perhaps we play God by condemning a broken life to a life of suffering.

Third, our God is a God of mercy and steadfast love. This is the bedrock of our faith, the mountain upon which we trod. Peter quotes David, "I saw the Lord always before me, for he is at my right hand, so that I will not be shaken. Therefore, my heart was glad, and my tongue rejoiced; moreover, my flesh will live in hope." (Psalm 16:8-9) "Moreover, my flesh will live in hope."

Peter writes again, "By God's great mercy he has given us a new birth into a living hope through the resurrection of Jesus Christ from the dead, and into an inheritance that is imperishable, undefiled, and unfading, kept in heaven for you." (1 Peter 1:3) Our God is a God of mercy and steadfast love. Our God is not a God of the CNN sound bite, the political posturing, the Internet blog-fest.

The question of a feeding tube is not an easy one to make. And there are many cases where, after much prayer, it is the right thing to do. But I am remiss that the media has cast the "religious" view as one where a feeding tube is mandatory. To decide against a feeding tube is thought to be un-Christian. I believe the issues are more complicated than a CNN sound bite.

And so, as your Pastor, let me put on the table, that a feeding tube, intubation, shocks and chest compressions, are not always the right and holy thing to do. As a Christian, you can decide against a feeding tube and still stand on sound theological principles. We are people of the resurrection. We are people of life, real life. Nothing separates us from the love of God. Our God is a God of mercy and steadfast love. This is Good News. Let us pray....

The Magi's Gift

In the time of King Herod, after Jesus was born in Bethlehem of Judea, wise men from the East came to Jerusalem, asking, "Where is the child who has been born king of the Jews? For we observed his star at its rising, and have come to pay him homage." When King Herod heard this, he was frightened, and all Jerusalem with him; and calling together all the chief priests and scribes of the people, he inquired of them where the Messiah was to be born. They told him, "In Bethlehem of Judea; for so it has been written by the prophet:

> *'And you, Bethlehem, in the land of Judah,*
> *are by no means least among the rulers of Judah;*
> *for from you shall come a ruler*
> *who is to shepherd my people Israel.'"*

Then Herod secretly called for the wise men and learned from them the exact time when the star had appeared. Then he sent them to Bethlehem, saying, "Go and search diligently for the child; and when you have found him, bring me word so that I may also go and pay him homage." When they had heard the king, they set out; and there, ahead of them, went the star that they had seen at its rising, until it stopped over the place where the child was. When they saw that the star had stopped, they were overwhelmed with joy. On entering the house, they saw the child with Mary his mother; and they knelt down and paid him homage. Then, opening their treasure chests, they offered him gifts of gold, frankincense, and myrrh. And having been warned in a dream not to return to Herod, they left for their own country by another road.

~ MATTHEW *2:1-12*

Holy God, The wise men took a risk, to follow your star, to follow your call. They sought a king and they found a purpose. They came to worship. They became transformed. Work in us with your Spirit, that we might be like those wise men. In Christ's name we pray, Amen.

Brothers and sisters, thank you for the honor and pleasure of worshipping with you all this morning. I realize that I am here under sad and uncertain circumstances: the illness of your pastor. While things are uncertain, I have made a commitment to be here with you all on the first Sunday of every month through June if you would have me. There are a few other Sundays sprinkled in. And so, I am glad to be here. I am committed to this. I am committed to you for the time we have together.

While many of you do not know me, I feel like I am old friend this congregation. I was the minister at East Pearl St. Methodist Church for 8 great years just down the street with a wonderful, loving, awesome group of people. I stepped down because my job jar at Yale was getting full. Christine and I had a second baby, and it was just too hard to be a solo pastor. It broke my heart when East Pearl closed a few years later. But we stayed in touch. I am here today because of three great pillars of the faith – Carol, Donna, and Queen Irene – who are now stalwart members here.

When I was at East Pearl St. Methodist, I had just gotten back from being a medical missionary in India and Honduras. All of my possessions could fit in the back of my 1984 Chevie. I had more hair. I was single, no kids.

At East Pearl, I "done growed up." I got married, had two kids – Eleanor and Evangeline - and moved up to Berlin Connecticut to live near my in-laws. When I started at East Pearl, I was a resident physician at Yale. If you watch shows like House or ER, I was one of those tired looking young-ish docs who were in training. When I left East Pearl, I was on the Yale Medical School faculty. I am now a middle-aged guy in middle manage-ment. I run a residency program and a clinic within the Yale system.

After East Pearl, I took a break from the ministry, and then joined South Church in New Britain as one of their associate ministers. I just stepped down a few months ago. I want you to know who I am, because I want to get to know who you are in the coming months.

For my adult life, I have been a "full-on" church guy. I love church. I love what churches do. I think church is the most beautiful, moving, spiritual moment of the week. I think church for many is the most intellectual mo-ment of the week. Church is the safe community where you can be your-self, where you are not judged, but welcomed by all.

The family of God can be the one place where you step outside of yourself and imagine what you are supposed to be. There is the family you are born into – you have no choice about that. Then there is the family that gathers you in – the church. My joy is with the Lord. My faithful walk is with Jesus Christ who saves me.

What we do here is important. We are a sanctuary of hope amidst the world that can be so hard and so difficult. I am committed to this. You, good people of St. Andrew's, have been this sanctuary. You model what it means to be the light of the world and the salt of the earth.

While I consider myself a church guy, a religious, spiritual, righteous dude, I realize that it might look like I represent that part of society that is not so religious or spiritual. I am a professor of internal medicine and pediatrics at Yale Medical School. I teach really smart young doctors about the evidence, the data, the logic behind making a diagnosis. Skepticism, critical analysis – that's what I teach. The ivy tower and the church steeple have not always been eye to eye (apologies about the odd the metaphor).

I share these two sides to my life, because these are the two sides to your life. Right? You have the deep yearning in your heart and you also have this this intellect integrity. You love, but in the modern world, you are also skeptical. Maybe even, we are a little bit jaded – jaded by all of it. Jaded by the rush of the holidays, jaded about our jobs, jaded about church, jaded about our crazy relatives, skeptical and uncertain even about ourselves.

This is why this Sunday is so important. This is the Sunday when we read the story of the Wise Men – the Magi – and how they journeyed to Bethlehem and discovered the Christ child. We call this day Epiphany Sunday, because this is the day of discovery.

Now here is the really cool part about Epiphany Sunday: the Magi are the modern people in the Christmas story. Here is what I mean: we do not know many details about the Magi, but we do know that they were astronomers. They measured the stars and figured out what it meant for their lives. They were learned. They were intellectuals. If the Wise Men were around today maybe they would work for Apple computer or be faculty at an ivy league university.

They were intellectual. They were also faithful. Their journey resonates with our own modern journey. They have much to teach us.

First, the Magi went on a journey. They took a risk. They left behind their old ways. Scholars think that the Magi traveled for years to get to Bethlehem. They did not have it all figured out. They merged their intellect and their faith together. I find that tremendously reassuring. God does not demand a perfect faith. God asks us to trust the star. They Magi did and it changed their lives forever.

Second, the Magi opened their hearts. In our modern days, it is trendy to skeptical, cynical about the world. But then you do not feel anything real. The skeptic will always be dissatisfied. It says in scripture,

> "There, ahead of them, went the star that they had seen at its rising, until it stopped over the place where the child was. When they saw that the star had stopped, they were overwhelmed with joy. On entering the house, they saw the child with Mary his mother; and they knelt down and paid him homage." (Matthew 2:10-11)

Joy. Worship. Love is always true, even though love is hardly ever reasonable. I will say that again: Love is always true, even though love is hardly ever reasonable. Think about all the crazy things you have done in the name of love. You can never convince a person through the power of argument about the existence of God. But, if you behold love, the power and presence of God is the most obvious truth in the universe. And what better way to behold love, than to behold a newborn baby.

Third, they gave of themselves. They brought gifts: gold for a king, frankincense because he would be priest, and myrrh to symbolize his death. Myrrh was used for embalming. They gave of themselves, because that's what you do when you know love.

Fourth, they returned by a different way. They changed. They were different people. Like Matthew writes, "And having been warned in a dream not to return to Herod, they left for their own country by another road." (Matthew 2:12) King Herod wanted to kill Jesus as a threat to his kingdom. After beholding Jesus, they were different people. Their allegiance was not to Herod, but to Jesus. Their allegiance was not to the powers of the world, but to the power of God.

The Magi: they went on a journey, they opened their hearts, they gave of themselves, and they were changed. The Magi: their faith and their intellect were one. That is the gift of the Magi: they show modern people that your reason can be faithful, and your faith can be reasonable.

There is one thing more: the Magi were outsiders. They came from the East. They were not Jewish. The shepherds were Jewish. Mary and Joseph were Jewish. Jesus was Jewish. As far as we know, the Magi were not Jewish. They were outsiders.

This is important because maybe you feel like you are an outsider. Maybe you feel like you are an outsider to church or an outsider to God. I am greatly comforted that the Magi were outsiders, and yet God game them a special role to discover God's purpose for the world. This special role now comes to you.

"Arise, shine, for your light has come, and the glory of the Lord has risen upon you." (Is 60:1) This great prophecy from Isaiah is the great gift of Epiphany, "Arise, shine, for your light has come, and the glory of the Lord has risen upon you." (Is 60:1) Amen.

Did Jesus Really Fly?

I have heard of your faith in the Lord Jesus and your love toward all the saints, and for this reason I do not cease to give thanks for you as I remember you in my prayers. I pray that the God of our Lord Jesus Christ, the Father of glory, may give you a spirit of wisdom and revelation as you come to know him, so that, with the eyes of your heart enlightened, you may know what is the hope to which he has called you, what are the riches of his glorious inheritance among the saints, and what is the immeasurable greatness of his power for us who believe, according to the working of his great power. God put this power to work in Christ when he raised him from the dead and seated him at his right hand in the heavenly places, far above all rule and authority and power and dominion, and above every name that is named, not only in this age but also in the age to come. And he has put all things under his feet and has made him the head over all things for the church, which is his body, the fullness of him who fills all in all.

~ EPHESIANS *1:15-23*

Holy and Loving God, bless these words, bless these our meditations, bless this gathering of your faithful, that, by your Spirit, You might deepen our faith, deepen our hearts to love. In Christ's name, Amen.

I need to ask the question, "Did Jesus really fly?" These are the passages that are traditional for Ascension Sunday. Today is the day in the church when we remember how Jesus left this world. Jesus did not ride off into the sunset like some cowboy. Jesus did not disappear in a cloud of smoke like some magician. How did Jesus leave this earth? He flew.

This question, "Did Jesus really fly?", is really a question about faith, biblical literalism, the role of science, and where your heart is with God.

Now, on a beautiful spring day, in our beautiful humble church, I want to talk about some weighty, powerful issues. "Did Jesus really fly?" is really a question about how you understand the Bible. Do you suspend reason for your faith?

For a modern person, the miracles in the Bible can be a stumbling block to the faith. The water into wine, the healing of the leper, the virgin birth and on and on – to the modern mind these miracles sound so incredible, so incredulous really, that it can be hard for a person to get past the miracles to get at who Jesus really was and what he did.

2,000 years ago, the miracles helped a person in their faith. Indeed, Jesus says over and over, "I do this so that they might know and that you might be glorified." A skeptic could look at Jesus, the one who healed the paralyzed man, and be affirmed in their heart that Jesus really had a holy power.

But these miracles are precisely what hold people back in their faith. "Aw, come on," a professor might say. "They are just a bunch of legends... Those events didn't really happen." If you let your mind get hung up on the miracles, then you miss the point of the Jesus who dies on the cross.

The image of Jesus ascending into heaven – Jesus flying – is a particularly powerful image. Superheros fly. We talk of Jesus as Savior, Shepherd, the Great Physician, Jesus-as-friend, Son of God, Son of

Man, Word-Made-Flesh. Jesus as Rabbi. Even Jesus-as-CEO. But Jesus as superhero is just too much. Jesus on ascension Sunday evokes a man with a blue suit with a red 'S' and long red cape. Jesus as superhero?

But is it possible to be a Person of Reason and a Person of Faith? Is it possible to believe that Jesus actually flew and also to believe in the laws of physics?

This is what I believe: what tips the balance between the mind and the soul is the heart. The mind understands this beautiful world. The soul aches for the tranquility of heaven. The heart loves. And in the loving heart, we find our faith and our reason. When it comes to miracles, faith, and reason, I want to highlight 5 points as a guide.

First, if you do not believe that Jesus flew, if you wake up one morning and your mind does not let your heart say, "yes" to the miracles, do not beat yourself up about it. Do not feel like you are a bad person, or a bad Christian. Do not hide from God, stop praying, feel guilty, stay away from church. Instead, sit in your doubt. Pray about it. Ask God. God will give you answers.

Second, if you do not believe in Christ's miracles, ask yourself this, "Is it the miracle or is it something else?" Are you getting in the way of your faith? Are you angry at God because you feel wronged, because something bad has happened to you. "Christ healed the blind man, but did not heal my husband," you might say. "Christ saved the little girl but did not save my daughter from the car accident."

Behind every intellectual argument, there is a bleeding, crying heart. Faith is an exercise in intellect, but it is never an exercise in intellect alone. Faith is about passion, imagination, and intellect. Listen to yourself. If you are angry with God, then put your anger to God.

Third, do not compromise your intellect, but do not let your intellect hold you back either. Let your heart have a say. Let your imagination have a say. In my younger days, I loved punching holes in Christian belief. In my younger days, I felt so enlightened and self-satisfied by pointing out how unreasonable Christ was. And maybe that's what held me back from enjoying God – my own arrogance.

I hold four degrees from Yale. I was a double major in biology and philosophy. But I realized that my life was missing something. My life was hollow without my faith. My life had no direction without my faith. Do not compromise your intellect, but do not let your intellect hold you back.

In the church, there is the line, "Faith seeking understanding." "Faith seeking understanding." I like that because it makes a point that our faith is always growing, always evolving, and always seeking understanding.

Fourth, do not lie to yourself. Do not blindly accept the miracles as true. Do not force the miracles into your mind. Do not let your soul beat down the importance of your mind. Accept yourself where you are. God responds to that. Thomas doubted. Peter denied Christ. Paul once persecuted Christians. But they all were honest with themselves. And God worked with them. God changed them. Shake an angry fist at God. Put your doubts before God. God will embrace you and love you for it.

To recap, first, do not beat yourself up about the miracles. Second, ask yourself why you do not believe in miracles. Third, do not compromise your intellect, but do not let your intellect hold you back. Fourth, do not lie to yourself. Do not let your faith beat down your intellect.

Fifth, let love guide your faith and your intellect. Christ came to your life to love you, to show you how much God loves you. Let love guide you. I love the line, "If you take a leap of faith, you discover that you can fly." I believe this to be true. "If you take a leap of faith, you discover that you can fly." Before the skeptics, before the great debates of our age, all God has to offer is the gift of love. All we have to offer the world, ultimately, is our ability to love.

The world is such a hard place. When we ask God, "Why do you let bad things happen?" I believe God asks the same thing of us, "Why do you, Ben Doolittle, let bad things happen?" "Why do you, good church folks, let bad things happen."

The world is a hard place. We know how hard life can be. How this city weeps for God's kingdom to fully come. How the children cry out for food and a safe home. Our hearts ache for the day when swords will be banged into plows. The world is hard.

I close with the words of Paul, in his letter to the Ephesians, which we read this morning. "I do not cease to give thanks for you as I remember you in my prayers. I pray that the God of our Lord Jesus Christ, the Father of glory may give you a spirit of wisdom and revelation as you come to know him, so that, with the eyes of your heart enlightened, you may know what is the hope to which he has called you, what are the riches of his glorious inheritance among the saints, and what is the immeasurable greatness of his power for us who believe." This is the good news. Amen.

God's Creation Plan for You

Now the eleven disciples went to Galilee, to the mountain to which Jesus had directed them. When they saw him, they worshiped him; but some doubted. And Jesus came and said to them, "All authority in heaven and on earth has been given to me. Go therefore and make disciples of all nations, baptizing them in the name of the Father and of the Son and of the Holy Spirit, and teaching them to obey everything that I have commanded you. And remember, I am with you always, to the end of the age."

~ MATTHEW 28:16 – 20

I want to talk about the Creation story, God's purpose in the world, and your role in it.

First the Creation story. Here is the scene. You are working at Walmart, going over your inventory. One of your buddies comes up to you and says, "You know Floyd, how can you believe in the Bible? I mean really, look at the creation story. How could that possibly be true? What about the Big Bang? What about Darwin and evolution? What about all the science that we know? How can you believe in the Bible?"

Maybe you are hanging out in the lounge in your apartment complex. Maybe you are walking from math class to history. Maybe you are playing the bagpipes in the rain on the train. You will have this conversation, "How can you believe in the Bible? Look at the creation story.... God made the world in seven days.... They didn't even have days and nights until the fourth day." All sorts of questions.

Maybe you have wondered the same question yourself, "I know that I am supposed to believe this story, but it just doesn't jive with how my brain is wired." I will tell you what I believe. I consider myself steeped in the scientific tradition. I have camped out in the lab. I went to medical school. I like to play with numbers and computers. A couple of months ago, I had a paper published in the *Journal of Clinical Investigation* devising a screening test for colon cancer.

So, when someone says to me, "Ben you are a doctor, how can you believe in the Bible?" When I am asked that question, I respond with a question, "How would a poet describe the Big Bang? How would an artist paint a painting of the universe? Is their interpretation any different from that of a scientist?"

A physicist takes a picture with a Hubble Telescope. A poet takes a picture with her imagination. My favorite story about the relationship between reason and faith is found in the annals of Star Trek. Dr. McCoy all fire and passion is dueling it out with the cool and calculating Dr. Spock. Finally, in exasperation, Dr. McCoy shouts, "You know Spock, sometimes you can't think your way to the truth. Sometimes you must love your way to the truth."

I am enough of a scientist to know that truth in science always changes. The earth was once the center of the universe, but we know otherwise now. What was there before the Big Bang, a scientist cannot tell you.

So, our science should not conflict with our faith. Rather, our faith and our reason can work together. We are human beings. We are not automatons. We have our reason. We have our imagination. To be faithful takes both.

So, is the story of God's Creation true? Yes. What is the truth that it tells us? I would say two things. First, the Creation story shows us that God is awesome. "In the beginning when God created the heavens and the earth, the earth was a formless void and darkness covered the face of the deep, while a wind from God swept over the face of the waters. Then God said, 'Let there be light,' and there was light."

"And God saw that the light was good; and God separated the light from the darkness. God called the light Day, and the darkness he called Night. And there was evening and there was morning, the first day."

This is awesome. God is awesome. God makes a dome in the sky. God pins the stars in the sky. God pushes fruit trees and sequoias from the ground. With a divine paintbrush, God paints autumn and spring and fall and winter. God is awesome.

"Let the waters bring forth swarms of living creatures, and let birds fly above the earth across the dome of the sky." And God looks at it all and says, "This is good. All of this is very good."

But God does not stop with creation. The second thing we know from the story of creation. You and I are made to have a plan in God's story of creation.

"Let us make Adamah in our image." "Let us make humankind, from Adamah" - which means earth or clay. God says, "I will make a people that look like me, and they are to have stewardship over all creation."

"I will make Carl, RJ, Irene, and Marion; and they shall have stewardship over my creation. Ginny, Marie, and Theresa will have stewardship over my creation. They will help in my kingdom. They will help in my world which I have created for them."

You have a role to play in God's kingdom. You have a role to play in God's plan. God is awesome. God made you. You are part of the divine, awesome plan of God.

The creation story is echoed in Christ's farewell story. "Listen to this," Jesus says. "All authority on earth and on heaven has been given to me. Go therefore and make disciples of all nations, baptizing them in the name of Father and of the Son and of the Holy Spirit and teach them to obey everything that I have commanded you. And remember, I am with you always, to the end of the age."

"God created humankind in God's image, and in the image of God he created them.... God blessed them, and God said to them, 'Be fruitful and multiply.... Have stewardship over the fish of the sea and over the birds of the air and over every living thing that moves upon the earth. I have given (everything) to you."

God entrusts human beings with the stewardship of the world. Christ, who has all authority, entrusts his disciples with the stewardship of the Holy Spirit."

You are part of the divine plan for God. Maybe you are thinking, "The rain has made my knees hurt." "I can't serve because of my troubles at home." "I am too tired on Sunday morning." "I am too sad to serve, too sick, too depressed." "I do not feel that I am important enough." "I do not feel like I have anything to offer."

If you are thinking those things, then I have news for you, good news for you. There is a place for you, a plan for your participation in the creation of God's Kingdom. You are important. You are needed.

Maybe your ministry is to make cookies, paint a fence, teach a child, and sing a song. Maybe your ministry is to visit the poor. Maybe your ministry is to be an example of kindness. Maybe your ministry is to pick up people who cannot come to church. Maybe your ministry is to pray, pray, pray. Pray for this church and all churches, pray for peace in this world.

God is awesome. God has made you. God has a purpose and plan for you in His Kingdom. This is the good news. Let us pray.....

Why Modern Medicine Needs St. Paul

*Now there was a disciple in Damascus named Ananias.
The Lord said to him in a vision, "Ananias." He answered,
"Here I am, Lord." The Lord said to him, "Get up and go
to the street called Straight, and at the house of Judas
look for a man of Tarsus named Saul. At this moment he is
praying, and he has seen in a vision a man named Ananias
come in and lay his hands on him so that he might regain
his sight." But Ananias answered, "Lord, I have heard from
many about this man, how much evil he has done to your
saints in Jerusalem; and here he has authority from the
chief priests to bind all who invoke your name." But the
Lord said to him, "Go, for he is an instrument whom I have
chosen to bring my name before Gentiles and kings and
before the people of Israel; I myself will show him how
much he must suffer for the sake of my name." So Ananias
went and entered the house. He laid his hands on Saul
and said, "Brother Saul, the Lord Jesus, who appeared to
you on your way here, has sent me so that you may regain
your sight and be filled with the Holy Spirit." And immediately something like scales fell from his eyes, and his sight
was restored. Then he got up and was baptized, and after
taking some food, he regained his strength. For several
days he was with the disciples in Damascus, and immediately he began to proclaim Jesus in the synagogues, saying, "He is the Son of God."*

~ ACTS 9:10-20

120

God of Grace and Glory and Love, you sent out your disciples and protected them with your Spirit on their journey. Work in us by these words and your love, that we might be encouraged by the faith. In Christ's name we pray, Amen.

The British Medical Journal published an article last month about "Retroactive Prayer."* What is *Retroactive* Prayer? In this study, they 3393 patient who had an infection in their blood – sepsis is what it's called. The study divided the group randomly into two groups. One group would get prayed for, the other *would not* get prayed for. The *retroactive* part is that these folks had already been in the hospital. Some had died. Some had lived. And there was a person designated to pray for half of them – after the fact. The study showed that there was no difference in mortality, but the folks who were prayed for had a shorter hospital stay and shorter duration of fever.

The British Medical Journal is the pre-eminent journal in England. It is akin to the New England Journal of Medicine or the Journal of the American Medical Association. My own career as a researcher and physician is notable for being rejected by the BMJ for a study I performed.

The folks involved in the BMJ are hard-core researchers, scientist-physicians who can crunch the numbers and care for the patients. So, I am amazed that these folks even entertain the subject of prayer and healing.

The article goes on to talk about Einstein's theory of relativity, Bosonic string quantum mechanics. The article quotes the physicist Stephen Hawking who said, "We've no idea how the world really is."

While the British Medical Journal is not a theological journal, nor does it have a Christian influence, the article does propose the provocative stance

* Olshansky, Brian, and Larry Dossey. "Retroactive prayer: a preposterous hypothesis?." *BMJ: British Medical Journal* 327, no. 7429 (2003): 1465.

that prayer makes a difference. The article suggests that physicians must keep our eyes open, and not be so stuck in their linear, rational world-view. The British Medical Journal subtly suggests this controversial vision (controversial at least for the BMJ) that you can, indeed, take some things by faith.

Now Saul had a vision problem. He had a vision problem at many different levels. One problem with his vision – his view on the world – is that he hated these new Christians and built his career around persecuting them. These followers of Christ were seditionists, traitors, rebels, doctrinal iconoclasts. Not to mention that, in the beginning, most Christians were of low state: the poor, the worker, the diseased, the outcast, the leper. Saul would easily dispose of these new followers of Jesus.

But, because of this vision problem – this world-view problem – Saul developed another vision problem: he was struck blind.

What happened on the Damascus road would leave the scientists at the BMJ babbling about Bosonic quantum string theory for weeks. There is Saul, a man of the Temple, a Roman citizen, on a crusade to Damascus to stamp out the infidels. Suddenly, a light blasts down upon him from heaven. He falls to the ground. He hears a voice come from heaven, "Saul, Saul, why do you persecute me?"
"Who are you?" asks Saul.
"I am Jesus." Says the voice from heaven.

Saul is struck blind. Although his eyes are open, he sees nothing. His companions lead him to Damascus where for three days neither eats nor drinks.

In Damascus, there was a disciple named Ananias, who is told by God, "Go, seek this man Saul, who is praying now, hoping to regain his vision, and lay hands on him."

Ananias says, "This guy Saul is one bad guy, are your sure?"

God says, "I have chosen him to be my instrument, my inside man, to bring my message to kings, to Gentiles, and to the Israelites."

Ananias finds Saul and lays hands on him. Immediately, scales fall from Saul's eyes, and he sees clearly. But more than that, he has a new vision on the world. And more than that, he has completely changed. He is a new person. In fact, he is so different that he changes his name from Saul to Paul. Immediately, he starts to proclaim Jesus in the synagogues preaching the good news of God's love in the world.

Jesus tells his disciples, "See, I send you out like sheep into the midst of wolves, so be wise as serpents and innocents as doves. Beware of them, for they will hand you over to councils and flog you in their synagogues; and you will be dragged before governors and kings because of me.... When they hand you over, do not worry what you shall say, for what you are about to say will be given to you at that time, for it is not you who speak but the Spirit of your Father speaking through you." (Matthew 10:16-18, 19-20)

What is this new vision that raises such anger in the world. Through Jesus Christ, God saves you from your sins. The challenge in our time is that no one really knows what that means anymore. Who is Jesus Christ? I am "saved"? From what? What is a "sin" anyway?

Another way of looking at it is this: Through Jesus Christ, you are changed, and made more holy, and made more whole. Your wrongs have been forgiven, but more than that, you are healed of all parts that are broken. You have worth – not because what you have done – but because how you are made.

In the year 2004, society looks at all that is broken and doesn't call it sin, we call it "dysfunction." We are in denial about our sin, not because we do not believe that sin exists – "don't lay a guilt trip on me" – but rather we doubt salvation. We doubt the power of God to change us. We doubt the love of God to save us. *That* is where we need a new vision.

How is your vision? Know this: Through Jesus Christ, God saves you from your sins. You are loved by Him and made like Him. This is the Good News. Amen.

Can Donatella Versace Juggle?

A certain woman named Lydia, a worshiper of God, was listening to us; she was from the city of Thyatira and a dealer in purple cloth. The Lord opened her heart to listen eagerly to what was said by Paul. When she and her household were baptized, she urged us, saying, "If you have judged me to be faithful to the Lord, come and stay at my home." And she prevailed upon us.

~ Acts 16:14-15

"Do you want to be made well? The sick man answered him, "Sir, I have no one to put me into the pool when the water is stirred up; and while I am making my way, someone else steps down ahead of me." Jesus said to him, "Stand up, take your mat and walk." At once the man was made well, and he took up his mat and began to walk.

~ John 5:6-9

I told my folks that I was preaching on Mother's Day – "Hey Ma, I'm preaching on Mother's day." Without missing a beat, in my mom's loving way, she says, "Oh, I had better come down to defend myself."

I remember another Mother's Day weekend a long time ago when my folks came down to Connecticut. They had come to visit me in medical school because, well, they were worried about their son. I had just completed my first year of medical school, just wrapped up final exams. The truth was that medical school had beaten me up real good. My body was suffering the toxic effects of gallons of coffee. Worse than that, my ego was suffering the toxic effects of too much medical school. "How could I possibly learn all this stuff?"

And so I skidded through finals with frayed nerves, wondering if it was all going to work out.

When Joe and Gay Doolittle found their son, he was unshaven, bleary eyed, with a pasty, sallow complexion. There was a pile of stinky, dirty dishes in the sink. The freezer had frosted over so much so that the door could no longer close. For some reason, it did not occur to me to defrost my freezer, maybe unplug the thing. Instead, I had positioned a chair in front of the freezer to keep the door partially closed. At the time, I thought this was a brilliant solution. Anyway, things were pretty bad.

My folks took it all in, and asked me how I was. As I was muttered my response, in mid-sentence, I closed my eyes, curled up into a ball, and fell asleep. I do not know exactly how long I slept, but when I awoke, the dishes were washed, dried, and neatly stacked. I heard the sound of a hammer banging away on something; it was my parents chipping ice out of the freezer. They had come to rescue their boy who had been beaten up by the world.

It was a moment that passed by without much reflection, but I realize now that it was a sacred moment, one of the millions of sacred moments that parents do all the time when they rescue their children. This is what incarnate love does. It is the sort of love that is not so much comprised of words but of actions. Love made real in the world. Love does many things, but maybe the first thing that love does is rescue the broken.

The two stories from this morning's lesson speak to the power of incarnate love. When we read scripture and we get to the geography in the Bible, we tend to blaze through it all – all the city's names and such. Our passage from the book of Acts has many small details that when we magnify them teaches us a lot about the power of the gospel.

Enter Lydia. She is from Thyatira, which is a city in what is now Turkey. Lydia, then, is Asian. It says that Lydia is a dealer in purple cloth, which means she is a business woman in the fashion industry. The story takes place in the city of Philippi, which is across the Aegan Sea in Greece. Philippi was an important Roman trading colony, a bustling place - think the garment district in New York.

So, not only is she a business woman, she is an *international* business woman. She must be successful because we know that she has a second house in Philippi. Today she would have her large home outside Paris and also a sensible brownstone on New York's upper east side. What is also significant is that she is a successful woman in a man's world. And so Lydia is remarkable – rich, worldly, fashionable, strong. She is intuitive and savvy enough to be successful across cultures. Lydia has it going on.

Here comes Paul. Paul is a Jewish priest, an intellectual, from the backwater of Palestine, the edge of the Roman Empire. He has spent his entire life steeped in Jewish traditions. My guess is that Paul knew nothing about the fashion industry of Asia Minor. And there are all sorts of rules about the decorum of a Jewish man speaking with a pagan, Asian woman.

Lydia, the sophisticated, fashion-savvy, business woman, and Paul, the zealot intellectual. What an odd encounter. What could they possibly have in common? What could they possibly talk about? Not only are they from different countries, Paul and Lydia are from different planets. It would be like Ben Doolittle having a conversation with Donatella Versace. Would she give me the time of day? What on earth would I say? "Hey, Sister Donatella, good cheer... Do you like to juggle?

There is one more thing that is important about Lydia. Lydia is looking for something. How do we know this? Because, outside the city walls, down by the river, Lydia, the pagan from Asia, is worshipping with the Jews. With all of her success, with all of her worldly achievements, she recognizes that there is something missing in her life. She needs to be there.

There are two things we do not know. First, we do not know what Lydia is missing from her life, but we can imagine. The fact that she so readily invites Paul and his crew to live with her makes me think that she is lonely. Her successful life demands sacrifice, months on the road, away from family. She trades the holiday at home for the business meeting with clients. She works late to keep the customers happy rather than deepening relationships with friends.

We know Lydia, because she is us. We know that for people to be really successful, all too often, something has to give, and all too often the casualties are those closest to us. With all the material success comes the regret of what could have been - friendships that did not deepen, conversations with loved ones that never occurred. All the purple cloth in the world cannot bandage those wounds.

The second thing we do not know is what Paul says to her. I would love to know. Who hasn't had the conversation with friends about the existence of God, who Jesus is, why we go to church? What do you say to Donatella Versace that makes her say, "C'mon everybody, come and live in my house."? I am sure that Paul's words are very wise, but I believe also that there is something else. An intellectual argument so rarely transforms the human heart. The journey from the head to the heart is the longest in the world.

I believe that in Paul, she finds her true home. There are all the pagan gods that demand all kinds of sacrifice. There is her job that demands all kinds of sacrifice. But in Christ, she discovers someone who makes a sacrifice for her. In Christ, she discovers an incarnate love that she does not need to broker or negotiate for. Before Christ, Lydia does not need to be the headstrong savvy business woman. She can be the vulnerable one who is rescued. At last, she finds her rest.

It is trendy to think that Christianity is for feeble-minded people. It is trendy to think that urban, sophisticated people would not be attracted to Christianity because it is somehow beneath them. This is why I think Lydia's story is so compelling. Here is a person who is one of the most worldly, sophisticated people we have encountered in the New Testament, and she really gets it. When you look at the history of the church over the centuries, the church always thrives in the major urban areas. The church thrives in the most multi-cultural places where there are widely competing ideas and different lifestyles. Ephesus, Thessalonica, Philippi, Rome... These are the places where the early church really took off. One reason the church thrives in the city is that people know how transforming it is to discover incarnate love, to have that experience of being rescued.

Jesus enters Jerusalem and encounters a paralyzed man, "Do you want to be made well?" I am so intrigued by the answer. The man does not say the expected such as, "Oh please Lord, for I am just so desperate." Or, "Please heal me for I am sick and tired of being sick and tired. I just need to get out of this place!" The man does not say these things. When Jesus asks him, "Do you want to be made well?" the man does not answer, "Yes, yes I do want to be made well."

Instead, he says, "Sir, I have no one to put me into the pool when the water is stirred up; and while I am making my way, someone else steps down ahead of me."

Huh? What does that mean? The tradition is that he first person in the pool gets the miracle. That is the tradition, but the paralyzed man does not answer the question. His non-answer is very telling. I think he is really saying, "I don't even know if I want to be made well again. I am too tired to hope. No one else cares enough about me. I can't even imagine what it would be like to be made well."

Jesus Christ, the Great Physician, says, "Stand up, take up your mat, and walk." At once, the man stands up, picks up his mat, and walks. He is rescued.

What does this story mean for you and me. This is what I believe. Maybe you would not put yourself in the category of the successful business person. Maybe you would put yourself in the category of this paralyzed man. Maybe you are so paralyzed in your life, so miserable, so beaten down, so utterly spent, that you cannot imagine what it would be like to walk. Maybe you are so crushed, so broken that you cannot even imagine what restoration would feel like, then I have news for you. Christ comes to rescue you. Even if you cannot imagine healing from whatever it is that has broken you, Christ knows your brokenness, because he was broken on the cross. In Christ, there is the power of God to rescue even you.

This is what the power of love incarnate in Jesus Christ does. This is what love does. For a beleaguered woman to recognize Jesus and for a paralyzed man to walk are both miracles that come from the same place: the power of God to rescue the broken. Jesus Christ says, "Stand up, take up your mat, and walk." With God's help, let us do so. Amen.

Wrestling with God

The same night he got up and took his two wives, his two maids, and his eleven children, and crossed the ford of the Jabbok. He took them and sent them across the stream, and likewise everything that he had. Jacob was left alone; and a man wrestled with him until daybreak. When the man saw that he did not prevail against Jacob, he struck him on the hip socket; and Jacob's hip was put out of joint as he wrestled with him. Then he said, "Let me go, for the day is breaking." But Jacob said, "I will not let you go, unless you bless me." So he said to him, "What is your name?" And he said, "Jacob." Then the man said, "You shall no longer be called Jacob, but Israel, for you have striven with God and with humans, and have prevailed." Then Jacob asked him, "Please tell me your name." But he said, "Why is it that you ask my name?" And there he blessed him. So Jacob called the place Peniel, saying, "For I have seen God face to face, and yet my life is preserved." The sun rose upon him as he passed Penuel, limping because of his hip.

~ GENESIS 32:22-31

Loving God, We gather in your house for a blessing and for bread. Bless these words and our meditations, that in receiving both, we would receive you. In Christ's name we pray. Amen.

I want to tell a story about making assumptions and challenging the status quo. The man's name is Ignac Semmelweis. The date, the mid-1800's. The place, Vienna, Austria. Ignac Semmelweis was an obstetrician. Early in his career, he was placed in charge of the birthing unit of the General hospital. This was a big deal. Vienna General Hospital was at the forefront of medical technology. Physicians came from all across Europe to study, learn new techniques, hear lectures from the most learned physicians in the world.

Dr. Semmelweis had a problem. His patients were dying. Women were dying. A lot of women were dying. At that time, if you delivered a baby in the Vienna General Hospital, you had a 20-30% chance of dying – that's 1 out of 5, maybe even 1 out of 3 mothers would die from overwhelming bacterial infections. No one could figure out why.

The one problem – quite an issue of pride actually – was that down the hall was the nurse mid-wife obstetrical unit. The mortality among the nurse mid-wives was around 3-5% - that's about 1 out of 20, 1 out of 30, mothers would die.

If you were lucky enough to deliver your baby at home, the mortality was only 1%. So, in the 1840's, in Vienna Austria, the last place you would want to deliver your baby was in the most prestigious hospital in all of Europe by the most learned of physicians. What was happening? What was going on?

Dr. Semmelweis noted that on the nurse mid-wifery ward, the mid-wives would show up early on the wards from their homes, and go about examining patients. The physicians would also show up early in the hospital. But before they rounded on patients, they performed autopsies on the patients who had died the previous day. After performing the autopsies, they would then go to examine the women and deliver the babies on the obstetrical ward.

Dr. Semmelweis had this idea that somehow the physicians were somehow infecting the patients. He instituted a policy. After performing the autopsies, you had to wash your hands. After examining each patient, you had to wash your hands. His superiors thought he was crazy. His professors were enraged at the audacity of the young doctor. Dr. Semmelweis stood firm. He instituted a policy. Everyone had to wash their hands. His colleagues scoffed at his simplistic view of the world. He endured the ostracism, the ridicule, the scrutiny of the medical community... until he began to save lives. Despite the overwhelming evidence, he was fired from his job and eventually was committed to a mental institution.

Of course, we now know that he was right all along. At the time, the establishment could not accept the radical new concept of "germ theory" and "infectious agents." The evidence was overwhelming, but the establishment could not believe it for themselves. Their assumptions blinded them to their reason.

We might look at this story and think, "How could those docs have been so blind, so dumb. It was so obvious from the beginning." But, these were the best physicians at one of the best hospitals in Europe.

This story is a mirror for our lives and our culture. *We* are modern people. Vienna, Austria in the 1800's was the most modern of places. *We* are sophisticated thinkers. *They* were sophisticated thinkers. I want to put out there that we do not wrestle with our assumptions.

The vanguards of old-school medicine could not bear to look at the truth because it would mean that thousands of women died at their hand. The stakes were too high. And so the establishment continued to live in denial. And thousands of people died because of it.

The assumptions and denial in our society – in our lives, yours and mine – have resulted also in the deaths of thousands. I think about how complacent we have become about the war in Iraq and Afghanistan: we are not angry enough. I think about how complacent we have become about how we treat the poor. Once we were a country where every home had a chicken in every pot. Now we expect a plasma screen TV – and we will gladly go into debt if we don't have one.

I want to think about Jacob as a modern person and look at his life as a mirror to our own. Jacob is a modern person. To recap his life: he is the younger twin to Esau, son to Isaac and Rebecca. Jacob chides his brother and tricks him out of his inheritance in exchange for a bowl of stew. Jacob tricks his father into blessing him, instead of Esau, when his father lies on his deathbed. That is the final straw. Esau threatens to kill Jacob.

So, Jacob flees to his uncle Laban's home. The soap opera continues. There, he works for 7 years to buy the beautiful Rachel as his wife. He is tricked into marrying Leah, Rachel's elder sister. He works another 7 years, finally marries Rachel. The chaotic family drama goes on and on. After 20 years, the family has become very wealthy, but Laban, his father-in-law, keeps Jacob under his thumb. Finally, Jacob has to get out of the house. He tricks his father-in-law out of much of the live-stock, and with nowhere else to go, he leaves in a big entourage across the desert to the only place he can imagine: home.

Jacob is a slick guy, a good talker, a grifter, a trickster. He spends his whole life answering the question, "What's in it for me?" Even though he was so self-centered many commentaries say that he still recognized the importance of God's blessings. He values the inheritance, the blessing from his father, the blessing from the man in the scripture today. I do not believe. I think Jacob approaches his spiritual life and his faith the way he approaches every other aspect of his life: "What's in it for me?" He does not ask for God's blessing so that he can live a more humble, more loving, more devoted life in service to God. He wants God's blessing the way he wants more sheep and more goats. This is a very modern, consumer-driven, consumption-oriented view of faith. "I want God to bless me. I want more stuff."

Something really powerful happens next to the river Jabbok. Jacob sends all of his flocks across the river. He sends his family across the river. The next day, he will face his brother. He does not know if Esau will kill him or not. For this last night, he wants peace and quiet alone.

What happens next is bizarre. A strange person emerges from the darkness. He has no name. He just appears. Jacob and the strange man start to wrestle. They fight all night long. In the struggle, Jacob realizes that this man is some kind of super-natural being, an angel, or maybe even God. As morning breaks, Jacob is not defeated.

The man asks Jacob, "What is your name?"

He replies, "Jacob."

The man says, "You shall no longer be called Jacob, but Israel, for you have striven against God and against humans and have prevailed."

Jacob asks him, "Tell me your name."

The man refuses to do so, but instead gives him a blessing.

In that blessing, something special happens. Jacob calls the place, "Peniel" which means, "I have seen God face to face." He wrestles with God and is a changed man. Something is different about him. But we don't know how different yet. He crosses the river. Later that day, he finally meets his brother Esau. There are tears of reconciliation, a long embrace, tears flow sweetly.

When he meets his brother, he says this, "If now I have found grace in thy sight, then receive my present at my hand, for therefore I have seen your face as though I had seen the face of God and you were pleased with me." "I have seen your face as though I had seen the face of God." Of course, Jacob *had* just seen the face of God. He wrestles with God and is so changed, is so different, that he no longer acts in a "what about me" personality. He looks at his brother and does not see a mark that he must win over. Instead he sees the image of God, an image which he recognizes.

What does this mean for us? If we wrestle with God, God wrestles with us, working us over. God will not crush us. God will change us. This is what I mean: we can be angry with God. We can serve up our fears, our doubts, our anxieties, our sins, God wrestles them all out us and makes us new, so that we can look at our brother and say, "I have seen your face as though I have seen the face of God."

This change in us happens though only when we face God, drop our assumptions, and be absolutely authentic with who we are. It is much easier to be a smug, self-satisfied agnostic, who is "spiritual but not religious." This person has never fully wrestled with God, because the stakes are too high. It is much easier to take on God on your own terms, as a "mark" to score, like Jacob scoring the blessing from his father. It is much easier to be lost to the world. But then, of course, you will never be changed. You will never see the image of God in the eyes of your neighbor.

As a Christian, I am not talking about wrestling with a nameless angel next to the Jabbok River, I am talking about wrestling with Jesus, and putting all of our doubts and anger and hang-ups and assumptions before him, and letting him change us.

We all need to come to terms with who Jesus is as modern people. The conservative church makes Jesus out to be the powerful Son of God, the Lord of Lords, the King of kings, the miracle-worker. What the conservative church loses is the humanity of Jesus, the one who is patient with the sinner and compassionate towards the outsider.

The liberal church is very comfortable with the servant Jesus, the one who reaches out to the leper and the blind. But the liberal church is uncomfortable with the idea that Jesus is the resurrected Son of God who has defeated death and sin.

I over-simplify "liberal" and "conservative" but I think there is some truth to this. Clearly, we need both – the servant Jesus and the Son of God.

I realize that the Bible can be a stumbling block to the faith. In particular, the miracle stories can be so troublesome to a modern intellect. The whole claim of the Bible is just so fantastic, so outrageous, how could it be true? That God the Creator becomes a man who serves you, loves you, heals you, dies for you, so that you can be forgiven of your sin, and live forever with God. This is an outrageous claim.

Feeding the 5000 with 5 loaves and 2 fish? Come on, how could that be true? I preached about this a few weeks ago, so will not spend too much time on this now other than to say that I believe that these miracles actually did happen. If you are the Son of God and want to reveal your glory, your power, your might in the form of a miracle, then do a real miracle: part the Red Sea, send manna from heaven, raise the dead, heal the blind. Do something impressive and fancy. But a picnic lunch? Bread and fish? It seems like such an odd miracle to make up. If you are going to lie about a miracle, lie about a really fantastic one.

For the sake of argument, let us put the issue of the miracle part of the story aside, and just look at what happened. 5,000 people let go of their assumptions, left their lives, and followed Jesus into the wilderness because something real was happening to them. Jesus healed the sick. Jesus proclaimed Good News. Jesus had compassion for them. Jesus changed their lives.

One last point. When we think about people in the Bible, we think of them as being superstitious and simple. This is simply not true. They were as jaded and ornery and suspicious as Viennese doctors in the 19th century or anybody else in any other century.

Do we have that courage that the Viennese doctors lacked? Can we really give up our doubts and fears to Jesus, so that Jesus can wrestle with us and make us new? It may be hard for our mind to contain this truth, but it is not hard for our heart. This is the work of grace. This is the Good News. Amen.

The Great Disconnect

The hour has come for the Son of Man to be glorified. Very truly, I tell you, unless a grain of wheat falls into the earth and dies, it remains just a single grain; but if it dies, it bears much fruit. Those who love their life lose it, and those who hate their life in this world will keep it for eternal life. Whoever serves me must follow me, and where I am, there will my servant be also. Whoever serves me, the Father will honor. Now my soul is troubled. And what should I say—'Father, save me from this hour'? No, it is for this reason that I have come to this hour. Father, glorify your name." Then a voice came from heaven, "I have glorified it, and I will glorify it again." The crowd standing there heard it and said that it was thunder. Others said, "An angel has spoken to him." Jesus answered, "This voice has come for your sake, not for mine. Now is the judgment of this world; now the ruler of this world will be driven out. And I, when I am lifted up from the earth, will draw all people to myself." He said this to indicate the kind of death he was to die.

~ JOHN *12:20 ~ 33*

Pray with me: Loving, wonderful God, you sent your Son to draw all people to you. By these words, our prayers, our worship, work in our hearts to draw us to you as your true children, beloved by you. May these words be yours, in Christ's name, Amen.

I want to talk about the National Institutes of Health, the "Great Disconnect", and the law of God. There is a common theme that brings these diverse topics together, so stick with me.

This past week I was in Washington DC at the National Institutes of Health for a conference on the interplay between Health and Spirituality. The nation's great researchers were there. One after another, they spoke of how important it is for a person's health to be religious, to practice regular prayer, to foster a relationship with God.

Herb Benson, a cardiologist and Director of the Mind-Body Institute at Harvard, spoke of the time when he brought people into his lab. He took folks, put an IV into their artery to measure blood pressure, strung up their heart and brain with electrodes.

He had people practice a centering prayer to speak the name of God over and over. Surprisingly (at the time), he watched their blood pressure go down.

Later studies showed that when people pray, stress hormones go down, relaxation scores go up. Researchers then decided that prayer is good for your health.

In the past 20 years, there has been study after study in the medical journals:
> If you go to church and have emphysema, you will live longer.
> If you become a patient in a Coronary Intensive Care Unit, and people pray for you, you will have a shorter stay, fewer complications, and have a greater chance of living.
> If you make less than 10,000 dollars/year, or
> if you are older than 75 years old,
> if you are recovering from a hip fracture,
> if you are a college student,

if you suffer from irritable bowel syndrome, arthritis,
AND you have an active spiritual life, you will have less depression
and improvement of symptoms, and even live longer.

One after another, researchers from our country's great institutions pre-sented their data. Religion is good for your health *and* your life.

When people say, "My church is the golf course…. I'd rather be a part of the Rotary Club: that's my church," the data show that actually it is church, NOT other civic groups, that bear out the positive health benefits. Researcher after researcher shared their data.

But here is the really interesting part: no one at the National Institutes of Health ventured to ask "why." What is special about religion and spirituality that gives a person all of these benefits? The "what" is the "what" that could not be spoken at the National Institutes of Health. No one could whisper the "what" in the halls of the National Institutes of the Health. Maybe researchers felt like they would not be taken seriously. Maybe researchers wanted to be polite in a multi-cultural, public setting.

What is the connection between health and spirituality? What?

The "what" is simply this: When Jeremiah prophesied, the people of God were struggling. The people of God – the Israelites – battled con-stantly. Invading armies threatened their homes, their children, and their very lives. Life is struggle. Life is a battle.

From the terror of their lives, Jeremiah said these words, "This is the cov-enant that I will make…. I will put my law within them, and I will write it on their hearts; and I will be their God, and they shall be my people. No longer shall they teach one another, or say to each other, 'Know the Lord,' for they shall all know me, from the least of them to the greatest… for I will forgive their iniquity and remember their sin no more." (Jer 31:33-34)

The "why" is simply this: God made us this way. God has written on our hearts a covenant, a promise, of love and forgiveness. God's promise is that God is very, very close, so close, so inside us, that we often overlook God.

I believe that in our lives we suffer from what I call, "The Great Disconnect." When we are 12 years old, we might not feel cool on the playground. We spend our time trying to be cool, trying to make friends. Sometimes it works. Sometimes it doesn't.

We grow up, look for a job, search for love, search for a home, trying to stay connected. We seek connection with other people, with ourselves, and ultimately with God. The loss of these connections is the "The Great Disconnect." The isolation. The doubt. The sorrow. The aimlessness. The drift. The sorrow. The depression.

To treat ourselves, we connect ourselves to emptiness: a bum relationship, a career, an outward appearance. We connect ourselves to emptiness. We connect ourselves to vapor. We connect ourselves to the past. We connect ourselves to the wind. And then we suffer the loneliness of "The Great Disconnect."

War is the ultimate disconnect, because we destroy all connections between people. Families are split apart so soldiers can fight. Homes are destroyed. Governments toppled. People die. People die. People die....

Jesus traveled to Galilee. There were Greeks there who asked, "We would like to see Jesus."

Jesus said, "The hour has come for the Son of Man to be glorified. Very truly, I tell you, unless a grain of wheat falls into the earth and dies, it remains just a single grain; but if it dies, it bears much fruit.... Now is the judgment of this world; now the ruler of this world will be driven out. And I, when I am lifted up from the earth, will draw all people to myself."

"And I, when I am lifted up from the earth, will draw all people to myself."

Jesus Christ, the law of God made flesh, comes into the world to draw all people to himself. He will die, but then he shall live. And so too will you.

Your sorrow. Your sin. Your loneliness. Your loss. Your grief. Your guilt. Your disconnect is reconnected. The "what" that folks at the NIH did not speak is Jesus Christ, the one who connects your heart, your life, your whole self to God.

Next week, we raise up our palm leaves in celebration of the Christ who comes into us, the law in our hearts, the Good News of God, the One who connects us and saves us. "And I, when I am lifted up from the earth, will draw all people to myself."
This is the promise. This is the Good News. Amen.

The Unifying Theory of Everything

From ages past no one has heard,
no ear has perceived,
no eye has seen any God besides you,
who works for those who wait for him.

You meet those who gladly do right,
those who remember you in your ways.
But you were angry, and we sinned;
because you hid yourself we transgressed.

We have all become like one who is unclean,
and all our righteous deeds are like a filthy cloth.
We all fade like a leaf,
and our iniquities, like the wind, take us away.

There is no one who calls on your name,
or attempts to take hold of you;
for you have hidden your face from us,
and have delivered us into the hand of our iniquity.

Yet, O Lord, you are our Father;
we are the clay, and you are our potter;
we are all the work of your hand.

~ ISAIAH 64:4-8

Loving, Wonderful God, move in us these cold days, that you would be a warm presence. Move in us, when the sun sets so early, that you

144

would light our path and illumine our hearts. Bless these words, O God, that they may be from you. In Christ's name, Amen.

I want to talk about the Fundamental Question of the Universe and the Extremely Simple Unifying Theory of Everything. Then I want to talk about advent and what it all means for our lives in the faith.

I discovered the Fundamental Question of the Universe and the Extremely Simple Unifying Theory of Everything in the New Yorker Magazine a few months ago.* When I saw the title, I was not sure if the article was about ethics or religion or maybe some mystical theology. Instead, the article was about physics.

Here is the big question in physics. On the one hand, there is the theory of relativity, which explains how planets and stars and galaxies all relate together. On the other hand, there is the theory of quantum mechanics, which explains how very small particles interact together. There are electrons, protons, and neutrons, but there are also quarks, gravitons, and these things called gluons and bosons (a boson sounds like a particularly dangerous and volatile creature indeed).

The problem is that no one has been able to figure out how the stars and galaxies relate with the bosons and gluons. How does the big relate to the small? There are people who stay awake at night worried about how gluons and galaxies work together. Maybe you have not worried about this, but there are some people who do.

There are physicists who ascribe to the string theory of the universe – the people who say the universe is made up of string. There are physicists who are in the loop quantum theory camp. Loops and Strings. Hatfield

---

* Wallace-Wells, Benjamin. "Surfing the universe: An academic dropout and the search for a Theory of Everything." *The New Yorker* (2008): 32-38.

and the McCoys. Capulets and the Montagues. Red Sox and Yankees. Two camps. Fundamentally different views of the universe.

Along comes a fellow named Garrett Lisi. He got his PhD in physics, but then dropped out of the academic grind. He spends most of his time surfing in Maui or skiing in Tahoe, working odd jobs to support his habit, and spending as much time as possible wrestling with the fundamental question of the universe. The amazing thing is that he has discovered it – or at least many people think so. He published his theory on the Internet, gave a talk at a big physics conference, and has set the physics world on fire. Of course, as soon as he published his theory, a legion of stringy physicists and loopy physicists gathered around to poke holes in his theory.

What I find so fascinating, so enthralling about this story, is this: their question, at the highest level of physics, was a question of faith. Is there order in the universe? Cloaked in this debate, using the language of mathematics is the fundamental question of faith – is there a unifying theory of everything or not? Is there order in the universe or chaos?

I am amazed that in the most rarified, arcane strata of the sciences, the whole discipline seems to rest upon faith. The question of the physicist is also our question. This modern question is also the question that grabbed the hearts of the early church. Is there order in the universe or chaos? Is God in control? How we answer this question has everything to do with how we live our lives.

I was saddened and horrified to hear of the tragic death of the gentleman working at Walmart in Valley Stream, Long Island, and this past Friday. As you may have heard, at 5am outside the Walmart, there were 2000 people pushing against the doors, anticipating the deals to be had. At 5:03am, the doors open. The crowd plows through and breaks the doors off their hinge. The man is pushed to the grown and trampled to death.

His death is a double tragedy. There is the loss of his life. The press is strangely silent about his identity. We do not know his name or if he had a family. The papers say he was working there through a temp agency. Was he between regular jobs? Was he having trouble making ends meet? We do not know. Yet, we grieve the loss of his life in such a tragic way.

There is the tragedy of his death. Then, there is the second tragedy. In our land of plenty, a crowd of people felt that they did not have enough. At a time when everyone is on a tighter budget, a crowd felt they had to spend more. And for what? To keep the kids happy with the new play station? To meet the expectations of a spouse? Was the money they saved worth more than the life of the man they trampled?

I share this story not to *implicate* the crowd, but to *identify* with the crowd. If I do not have faith in the Son of Man coming in power and glory to rescue me, then I must do something to give me structure, stability, and comfort. If I do not have the faith that I will have a job in January, then I must place my trust in what I can see and touch and hear. I surround myself with *things*. The crowd who cheered for Jesus on Palm Sunday was the same crowd that shouted, "Crucify him," on Good Friday. What happened at that Walmart goes way beyond simple materialism. It's much deeper than that. The stampede of that crowd was born from fear in what they believed to be an unstable and unfair universe – a universe where the quantum loops and strings strangle you, where the quarks and gluons spin out of control and make life chaotic and uncertain.

The prophet Isaiah gives voice to the doubts and worries of a struggling people, "O that you would tear open the heavens and come down, so that the mountains would quake at your presence.... When you did awesome deeds that we did not expect, you came down, the mountains quaked at your presence.... (Yet) there is no one who calls on your name, or attempts to take hold of you; for you have hidden your face from us, and have delivered us into the hand of our iniquity. Yet, O Lord, you are our Father, we are the clay, and you are the potter, we are all the work of your hand." (Is 64:1, 3, 7-8)

Isaiah's cry is an honest one, "Come down God, so that I can see you. It is not enough that you are the God of the Universe; I need you to be the God of Right-Here-Right-Now. Let the universe take care of itself, I have bills to pay and children to clean up after. My parents need me and work is so hard."

And yet at the end of Isaiah's tirade, there is a forlorn, whispering hope, an earnest prayer, "Yet, O Lord, you are our Father, we are the clay, and you are the potter, and we are the work of your hand."

"I might not know you, but you are our Father, and we are in your hands. Shape us. Mold us. Take us. Make us truly your own." That is an honest prayer that makes sense to me. It is infinitely better to have a weak faith in something strong than a strong faith in something weak.

The early Christians had a dilemma. The Gospel of Mark was first circulated around 50-60 AD, about 20 to 30 years after the Jesus' crucifixion. This means that the people who heard this scripture had probably heard a lot about Jesus, but probably had never met him first-hand. Jesus' memory would have been fresh in the minds of the people, but secondhand. Jesus' language is strong and clear: "I am coming." And yet, when?

"Truly I tell you, this generation will not pass away until all these things have taken place. Heaven and earth will pass away, but my words will not pass away. But about that day or hour no one knows, neither the angels in heaven, nor the Son, but only the Father. Be aware. Keep alert; for you do not know when the time will come." (Mark 13:30-32)

There is a Unifying Theory of Everything. The God of the Universe does become the God of the Right-Here-Right-Now. The One who shakes the heavens and sends out the angels also comes as a child. It is easy to love a baby, any baby. In that love, you can imagine the angels singing alleluias. That bundle of love in your arms is real and smells nice and loves you back.

Despite the skepticism and the materialism and all the jaded sentiments of our age, at the end of the day, I believe it is easier to trust God's love than it is to trust stuff from Walmart. Even though the Gospel of Mark tells me to "keep awake," I find it more sensible to trust a distant God who comes near to us, than it is to trust a stock portfolio. To have faith can be hard in the year 2008. Yet, I believe it is infinitely better to have a weak faith in something strong than a strong faith in something weak. God, who is the potter, can take our doubts and turn them to strengths.

We may not understand what a boson or a gluon does, but we can imagine what it feels like to be loved. And that, brothers and sisters, is the unifying power of the universe. Thanks be to God, Amen.

Hoping

Heroin and the Gospel of Hope

Now he was teaching in one of the synagogues on the Sabbath. And just then there appeared a woman with a spirit that had crippled her for eighteen years. She was bent over and was quite unable to stand up straight. When Jesus saw her, he called her over and said, "Woman, you are set free from your ailment." When he laid his hands on her, immediately she stood up straight and began praising God. But the leader of the synagogue, indignant because Jesus had cured on the Sabbath, kept saying to the crowd, "There are six days on which work ought to be done; come on those days and be cured, and not on the Sabbath day." But the Lord answered him and said, "You hypocrites! Does not each of you on the Sabbath untie his ox or his donkey from the manger, and lead it away to give it water? And ought not this woman, a daughter of Abraham whom Satan bound for eighteen long years, be set free from this bondage on the Sabbath day?" When he said this, all his opponents were put to shame; and the entire crowd was rejoicing at all the wonderful things that he was doing.

~ LUKE 13:10-17

Wonderful God, moved with compassion, your Son set free a woman who was so severely afflicted. By your grace, we pray that you would set *us* free from our afflictions. Bless these words, that they might be yours. Bless our thoughts that they might come from you, strengthening our faith. In Christ's name, Amen.

Two blocks from this sanctuary, a young man has just bought a bag of heroin. One bag of heroin costs about 10 dollars. If you buy 10 bags – which is called a bundle – you get a discount. A bundle of heroin costs about 60 dollars, maybe 70.

In my life as a physician, in the clinic where I work, I treat people addicted to heroin. There is a medicine called buprenorphine I prescribe which blocks down the drug receptor and makes the cravings go away. I have learned much about this world – this world of the drug addict. The demon of heroin addiction has become a daily specter in my professional life.

I realize that heroin may be an unusual topic for a sermon, but if you look at the numbers – and throw in cocaine addiction and alcoholism – chances are drugs have touched your life or someone you love.

The best thing about heroin is also the worst thing. If you take that bag of heroin, snort it, smoke it, or inject it, all of your problems go far, far away. For 10 dollars, all of your problems go away. A bargain. Your lousy job, gone. Your busted up relationship, gone. That horrible trauma from your childhood, gone. That nagging guilt from the mistake you made, gone. The shame, gone. All of it is gone. Completely gone. Drugs work.

A bag of heroin is good for about an hour or two. To live your life completely in a state of altered consciousness, you need about 10 bags of heroin a day.

The best thing about heroin is also the worst thing. I am about to state the obvious, but I want to frame it in a way that is maybe a little different. Here is the problem with drugs – you do not lose your problems, you lose yourself. The drug that was your escape from your problems becomes the problem itself. You lose your life to the drug, and the drug becomes your life. You become a slave.

And suddenly, every fiber of your being, every waking moment, every thought, and every breath is focused on getting the next hit. The addict becomes supremely self-absorbed. The addict will do anything – sell her mom's jewels, prostitute herself, anything. But in becoming self-absorbed, the addict loses himself. The addict becomes a slave to the drug. The drug becomes the false god that says, "Give me your life, and I will reward you. I will make you feel better." You become a slave to a false god, and the appetite of a false god is insatiable.

Maybe right now some of you are thinking, "Phew! I am glad I'm not a heroin addict." But, I think you can also see that what I am talking about goes way beyond heroin, and even beyond addiction – alcohol, crack. I am talking about slavery.

There is a lot of other stuff besides drugs that enslaves us, isn't there? A lot of it is very subtle. Are you a slave to your job? Are you a slave to what other people think about you? Would it mortify you if your neighbors had a bad opinion of you? Are you a slave to your stuff? Are you a slave to your credit card bill?

Have you lost yourself to grief? Does a horrible memory enslave you? Will you never be at peace in your heart because of something you have done?

Here is the question for us, "Is Jesus more compelling than heroin?" Is our faith enough for us to overcome our addictions, our enslavement? I know we are *supposed* to believe it does, but do we *really* believe it? Is religion better than heroin?

Recently, I discovered a really great book called <u>Blue Like Jazz – Irreligious Thoughts on Christian Spirituality</u>. I would put Donald Miller, the author, in the category of "post-modern apologist." He explains the Christian faith to a society that has grown jaded and tired of "traditional religion." He writes,

"Everybody wants to be fancy and new.... One night, when I was watching television, I saw an infomercial about a knife that could cut through a boot and remain sharp enough to slice a tomato. They called it the Miracle Blade. Another night I saw a cleanser made with orange juice that could get blood out of carpet. They said it worked like magic. The whole idea of everybody wanting to be somebody new was an important insight in terms of liking God. God was selling something I wanted. Still, God was in the same boat as the guy selling the knives. .... Everybody exaggerates when they are selling something. Everybody says their product works like magic. At the time (and he was early in his Christian journey) I understood God's offer as a magical proposition, which it is. But most magical propositions are just tricks. The older you get, the harder it is to believe in magic. The older you get, the more you understand there is no Wizard of Oz, just a (guy) behind a curtain."[*]

If our faith is a "trick" or "magical proposition" – like a Ginsu knife or a miracle cleanser – then it is not enough. Heroin is more compelling than faith. If our God is just a guy behind a curtain, then the white powder will do just fine, thank you very much.

If we look at the stories in the Bible and what Jesus did, we can ask the question, "Who comes to Jesus?" Who really comes to Jesus? The answer is: the slaves. Those who have lost something. All who are outsiders. All who have problems bigger than themselves. The Ethiopian Eunuch, the Roman Centurion when his son dies, Martha and Mary when they lose their brother Lazarus, the man with the shriveled hand, the paralyzed fellow who gets lowered through the roof, Matthew the tax collector who is disenfranchised from society. The woman in our Gospel passage this

* Miller, Donald. *Blue like jazz: Nonreligious thoughts on Christian spirituality*. Thomas Nelson Inc, 2012, page 29.

morning who was crippled. When Jesus laid hands on her, we read that, "She stood up straight and began praising God."

These are the people who understood what Jesus was doing for them. Only a slave can know how precious, how sweet, it is to be free. Only a sick person can imagine how unbelievably wonderful it would be to regain health again.

Who are the people who do not come to Jesus in Scripture? Who does not "get it?" All the people who are so confident that they have it all figured out. When Jesus heals the woman in our passage this morning, the Pharisees are furious, incensed, offended that Jesus would work on the Sabbath. The Pharisees did not get it. They did not get that religion – real religion – is not about rules, but about life.

When this passage comes up in Bible study and in sermons, often we dwell on Jesus healing on the Sabbath, doing work on the Sabbath, and violating Jewish law. While that is not untrue, I think this passage is about slavery. Who is the slave in the passage? The Pharisees.

The Pharisees are easy marks for us to judge them, but they were slaves and addicts just like we are. They were slaves to their rules and they did not know it. So, when Jesus came into their lives, they could not fathom what he could do for them.

There is one small detail to the Gospel passage that often goes missed. In other healing passages, people often cry out for Jesus for healing. "Only say the word, and my servant will be healed." (Matthew 8:8) In this case, the woman did not ask to be healed. She was just there. Jesus calls to her, lays hands on her, and heals her. Sometimes we seek God. Sometimes God reaches out to us without our knowing.

I have three final thoughts:

First, the only way to really beat addiction, to overcome slavery, is through the grace of God. I do not say this in a glib info-mercial sort of way. The only way to beat addiction is through God working in our heart, moving in our minds, making us new. By definition, an addiction has more power over you than you can shake off by yourself. The pills are never enough. Only by grace do we become new creations. Only a power greater than ourselves, greater than our addictions, can break the bonds of slavery.

One place where this power lives is here – this church – the body of Christ on earth. God works through people, through you, through this place, in friendships, in prayer, in love, to make people new. I believe this place is our great blessing and also our great work.

Second, until we see in ourselves how we are slaves to our false gods, we will never really understand – intellectually and spiritually – how powerful Christ can be in our lives. Until we see how we are slaves, Christ will not mean much, because the stakes in our own lives are not high enough.

Third, the difference between heroin and Jesus is that heroin is a false god and Jesus is the living God. A false god says, "Give me your life, and I will reward you." This is a lie: the appetite of a false god is insatiable, and will always demand more and more. Jesus, the living God, says, "I will give you my life, and you will be my reward." "I will give you my life, and you will be my reward." Amen.

Milk, Milk, Milk

Is there no balm in Gilead?
Is there no physician there?
Why then has the health of my poor people
not been restored?

~ JEREMIAH 8:22

And I tell you, make friends for yourselves by means of
dishonest wealth so that when it is gone, they may wel-
come you into the eternal homes.

~ LUKE 16:9

God of Love and Power, You call us to serve you and no other. By your grace, bless these words that they would be yours, that you would strengthen us in the faith, encourage us in our holy work. In Christ's name, Amen.

I want to tell you a story about money.

I am in Calcutta, India. The year – it was a lifetime ago. I have just finished several months working as a doctor in a rural village in the south, and it is time to head home. Before I leave India, I want to see a bit of the sites. I am a pilgrim, of sorts. I go to Calcutta. I seek the home of Mother Theresa.

Calcutta is a city of pilgrims and refugees from Bangladesh and the surrounding villages. I am merely one more. I get off the train. Calcutta is a city built on a swamp. I am swept into a morass of traffic, coated in a blanket of languid dust and wheezing heat, a stench of gasoline and spices. It is great.

I hitch a ride over the bridge, and stash my bag in a flop-house. I open my guidebook, just another pilgrim, looking for a golden coin. A refugee in search of refuge. The refuge that I seek is, of course, the Mother House of Mother Theresa. I open my guidebook. I am really more of a tourist, I realize. I want to stand in the doorway of the Mother Ship, the Mother House of the Sisters of Charity. Mother Theresa's troops. Mother Theresa, who gave out golden coins of hope and love to Calcutta's refugees and pilgrims. I am a groupie, a fan. I want to visit the Palace where her Empire of Compassion began.

She had died a few months before and I wanted to stand in the cloud of her powerful memory, absorb her somehow, and become more like her. I walk where she walked, down the narrow streets, guide-book open to the map, past the fruit stalls, the sewers, the mothers bathing their children on the side-walk, the rickshaw wallahs pulling their customers through the chaotic streets.

I am closer now, closer, nearly at the dot marked "Mother House" on my map. I walk past a motorcycle fix-it shop, a gray 2-story warehouse, the local chapter of the Indian Communist Party, a bread store, and then I am nowhere. I am on a bridge at a busy intersection. I have passed Mother Theresa's House. I missed it somehow.

From the corner of my eye, I see two nuns fly out of the alleyway next to the gray warehouse. I backtrack and look up to see a simple, bronze plaque on the wall, green with age - "Missionaries of Charity." The Palace for Mother Teresa's Empire of Compassion is a two story, gray warehouse.

In my heart, I expected something more – maybe a Disney-like castle with a neon sign. But really, a refitted warehouse makes perfect sense. She is a woman who traded her Nobel prize dinner for rice and beans for the poor.

I am standing on the street corner, taking it all in. I feel a tug on my wrist. Before me is a thin girl, maybe 12 years old. She wears a blue dress, a little worn, but clean. She has a twisted right hip and a spastic arm. I brace myself for she is the one-millionth person to ask me for money that day.

"What is your name?" she asks. She is cheerful and friendly, and addresses me as if we were at a church barbecue.

"I am Ben. What is your name?"

"I am Molly. Buy me some milk. Milk. Milk. Milk." Not a request. A command.

In the shadow of Mother Theresa's home, how could I say no? I follow Molly as she limps to the grocer. "Milk. Milk. Milk," she commands.

The grocer places a large box of instant dry milk on the counter. "300 Rupees," he says. I balk.

"300 rupees?" That is almost 10 American dollars and more than I spend on food in a week on the road. I do some math. I have just over 80 dollars worth of rupees, and 5 more days of travel. It would be very tight indeed.

"Milk. Milk. Milk," smiles Molly.

"300 Rupees! Too expensive!"

"Milk. Milk. Milk."

"No Milk! No Milk! No Milk!" Perhaps I am too tired, too cheap, too rational, too beaten down by trail. The flood of excuses and rationalizations tastes like bile, but I do not yield. "What good will this do her in the long run," I think to myself. But this time it's different, and somehow I know it.

It is over before I can change my mind. Molly looks at me. She smiles. She turns and melts into the crowd. She is gone. The angel with the twisted hip disappears. I am left with the taste of bile and regret. The devil smiles. Milk. Milk. Milk.

Hear the word of God from the prophet Jeremiah, "For the hurt of my people, I am hurt, I mourn, and dismay has taken hold of me. Is there no balm in Gilead? Is there no physician there? Why then has the health of my poor people not been restored?" (Jer 8:21-22)

Why? Because the physician just stood there and made excuses.

"O that my head were a spring of water, and my eyes a fountain of tears, so that I might weep day and night for the slain of my poor people." (Jeremiah 9:1)

Milk. Milk. Milk.

I remembered this story as I read the parable today. There are two kinds of passages in the New Testament – the easy ones and the hard ones. The easy passages are the ones we memorize in Sunday School – "The Lord is my shepherd," "The Good Samaritan," "Blessed are the peacemakers, for they shall inherit the earth." These are the passages that we lean on in times of trouble. These are the passages of comfort.

The hard sayings are important for a different reason. The hard sayings in scripture make us slow down and read the text carefully. What does Christ mean in this parable? When we slow down, we let God work in us more thoroughly. This parable is a hard one, and there is a lot going on.

To recap the story: there is a manager of an estate. The landowner wants to fire him because he does such a bad job. Catching wind of this, the manager sits down with the landowner's debtors.
"You owe 100 jugs of oil. Take your bill and make it only 50."
"You owe my boss 100 containers of wheat. Sit down and pay me only 80."

He cuts a deal to make some friends. He is networking for his next job. When the landowner gets wind of this, he is not angry. Instead, the landowner praises him. And Jesus says, "Make friends for yourselves by means of dishonest wealth so that when it is gone, they may welcome you into the eternal homes." (Luke 16:9)

What is going on here? Does this parable let crooked hedge fund managers off the hook? "Make friends with dishonest wealth?" Does this mean Tony Soprano has been right all along? Is this finally the biblical justification for cheating on our taxes?

This parable becomes more clear with the last line, "No slave can serve two masters; for a slave will either hate the one and love the other, or be devoted to the one and despise the other. You cannot serve God and wealth." (Luke 16:13)

Milk. Milk. Milk.

I have read all sorts of commentaries about this parable, and there are all sorts of intellectual gymnastics and clever exegesis. But when I remember Molly with the twisted hip, I understand what this parable means. This is what I believe: God is more important than money. People are *always* more important than money. This sounds simple, but it is hard to keep our priorities straight.

The more we pursue money in the heart, the more that money has dominion over us, then the more lost we become. If we love money more than God, we lose ourselves to the rat race, the career path, and the crush of workaholism. Our friendships, our marriages, our relationships, our churches, our faith all suffer. And we shall know the bitter isolation and loneliness that pains our society today.

We live in a society that has lost its soul to money and we see the casualties on every page of the newspaper – the corporation that refuses to give health insurance, the sub-prime loans and the swindlers who brokered the deals. Did a bigger house make them happier? Was I more secure with 10 dollars in my pocket?

Like Mother Theresa said, "Being unwanted, unloved, uncared for, forgotten by everybody, I think that is a much greater hunger, a much greater poverty than the person who has nothing to eat…. We must find each other."

A doctor and a beggar stand on a street corner in India. Who is lost? Who is found? If we love God more than money, God shapes us and we walk in this world with a confidence, a comfort, a security that no money can buy. We know where we stand.

I kept 10 dollars because I thought that giving it away would break me. Yet, those 10 dollars *did* break me, precisely because I *did not* give it away. At the end of the day, it is not about money, but it is about trust. I do not understand my computer, but I trust that it will work. I know how God works better than I know how my computer works: I can trust God more than I can trust my computer.

If you have ever been in love, you realize that you cannot know everything about your beloved, but you love that person anyway. The same is true for God. God does not ask us to have every detail figured out. God asks us to trust.

You came to church today. A girl with a twisted hip and a blue dress stands before you. "Milk. Milk. Milk." You are tired. You have seen it all before. Yet, the whole world is before us. The whole world is before our church. The world is thirsty for milk. The hurting world cries out, "Is there a balm in Gilead?" The world aches for God. This is our moment. Our time is now. There she stands, and she asks you for milk. What do you do?

Hope in the Long Days of Darkness

The people walking in darkness have seen a great light. On those living in the land of the shadow of death, a light has dawned. For to us a child is born, to us a son is given, and the government will be upon his shoulders. And he will be called Wonderful Counselor, Mighty God, Everlasting Father, Prince of Peace.

~ ISAIAH 9:2, 6-7

Loving, Wonderful God, let it be so in us that this Christ child, would be born anew in us. Deepen our faith. Make bold our love. Bless us all in the hearing of these words and in our deepest meditations and desires, that they may be yours. In Christ's name, Amen.

An article in the New York Times caught my eye. The title of it was, "Doctors' Delicate Balance in Keeping Hope Alive."* The article tells of the challenge that doctors face in conveying hope to their patients in dire circumstances. There is "false hope" where the doctor says that everything will be well, when, in fact, it will not. At that same time, there is "false hopelessness" when things are not so dire as they appear.

Certainly this article grabbed my attention because of my other role in the world, I was impressed that the New York Times wrestled with something that is so much at the core of being human – hope – that is so much a part of a family's life – dealing with illness.

---

* Hoffman, J. (2005). Doctors' delicate balance in keeping hope alive. *The New York Times*, 12, 24.

Here is the story from the New York Times, and I quote:

"Robert Immerman, a 56-year-old Manhattan architect, knew that his brain cancer - a glioblastoma, Grade 4 - meant terrible news. After the tumor was removed, he asked the radiation oncologist his prognosis.

"The doctor was pleasant," Minna Immerman recalled, "as if he was telling you that hamburger was $2.99 a pound. He just said the likely survival rate with this tumor was, on the outside, 18 months.

"Bob purposely forgot it," she said. "I couldn't."

After radiation, Mr. Immerman began chemotherapy. But after one treatment, his white blood cell count dropped so precipitously that it was no longer an option.

"The medical oncologist said, 'The chances of survival with or without chemo are very, very slight,' " said Mrs. Immerman, a special-education teacher. "I think she was trying to make us feel better. What I heard was: 'With or without chemo, this won't end well, so don't feel so bad.' "

Mr. Immerman got scans every two months. Mrs. Immerman watched the calendar obsessively. Twelve months left. Six months.

"As time passed, instead of feeling better, I felt like it was a death sentence and it was winding down," she said.

She sweated the small stuff: should they renew their opera subscription?

Mr. Immerman turned out to be one of those rare people who reside at the lucky tail end of a statistical curve. In February, it will be 10 years since he learned his prognosis. He is well. For years, Mrs. Immerman was shadowed by fear and depression about his illness, before she finally allowed herself to breathe out with gratitude."

Hope in medicine, for a doctor, a scientist, maybe even a friend, is built upon probabilities. "What does the data say?" "What do the studies show?" An atheist can only share the odds. Life is messy and it is a crapshoot, and so the conventional wisdom of our society is not very wise at all. In the midst of suffering, the modern world can only give platitudes. "Keep a stiff upper lip." "Things will get better." "All things work for the best." Empty words most of the time. In a secular, New-York-Times kind of hope, the big question is "What do you hope for?" "In what do you have hope?"

Hope for a Christian is a lot more than a New York Times-kind-of-hope. In the story of who Jesus Christ is, our hope *points to something*. All the world will give platitudes, but in our faith, our hope grows from deep roots. Our hope grows from the power of God.

Isaiah told the whole world, "The people walking in darkness have seen a great light. On those living in the land of the shadow of death, a light has dawned. For to us a child is born, to us a son is given, and the government will be upon his shoulders. And he will be called Wonderful Counselor, Mighty God, Everlasting Father, Prince of Peace." (Isaiah 9:2, 6-7)

What is powerful is that the Christ-child had not yet been born. Jesus was born several hundred years later, but Isaiah speaks as if it has already happened. "The people walking in the darkness have seen a great light. (This has already happened) One those living in the land of the shadow of death, a light has dawned. For to us a child is born (this has happened), to us a son is given, and the government shall be upon his shoulders."

For Isaiah, the truth of God was so powerful, so real, that Christ-child was born already in his heart and his mind, even though temporally, the world would know of Jesus many years later.

Here is the good thing about hope: you don't have to be perfect to have it. You don't need a perfect faith (whatever that is). Your faith need not be pigeon-holed into some tidy doctrine. You don't need straight A's in moral behavior. You don't need the pedigree of an aristocrat or be connected to the right politician.

What I believe we need to do is what the shepherds did. We need to walk. We need to seek. We need to be in touch with our hearts in what we really, really need. When the angels flattened those good shepherds with light and power and love, they said, "Let us now go unto Bethlehem, and see this thing which is come to pass, which the Lord hath made known unto us." They did not intellectualize. They did not theorize. They did not offer empty platitudes. They came to see for themselves.

When they beheld the Christ child in a manger, wrapped in bands of clothe, in the company of the cows and the sheep and the angels, they knew instantly that this was the Son of God. Their hopes were realized. The hope bore the fruit of faith, and they were never the same again.

Our lives are messy and complicated – at least, I suspect, as messy and complicated as a shepherd living under the oppression of the Roman government and the rule of Pharisees. The suffering of our people has been very great in recent months. And yet, you all came here tonight, on a cold dark night in midst of it all. You did what the shepherds did: you came to see for yourselves. God will do the rest.

P.U.S.H. Pray Until Something Happens

"Peace I leave with you; my peace I give to you. I do not give to you as the world gives. Do not let your hearts be troubled, and do not let them be afraid."

~ JOHN 14:23-29

Wonderful, Holy God, your Peace you give to us. You come to us as Advocate, Counselor, a Loving Presence. Alight your Spirit upon us, that we might be fortified by your love, and come to believe in your power. Bless these words that they may be yours. In Christ's name, Amen.

I want to tell a story about the last time I punched someone in the chest. When was the last time you punched someone? This is a story about a change of heart. This is a true story. The past two Sundays I have not been here, because of my duties as a doctor in the Medical Intensive Care Unit at St. Mary's Hospital. This is a job that makes my stomach churn in knots.

"Doctor Doolittle, come to the next room. The man in room 36 is in V-tach."

V-tach. Ventricular tachycardia is a kind of heart rhythm. On the monitor, the heart rhythm looks like a row of jagged shark's teeth. The heart beats in a disorganized way. Blood cannot flow through the chambers normally. It is a heart rhythm that causes death. People die when their hearts flips into V-tach. The man in room 36 was about to die.

There are three things you can do. One treatment for V-tach is to give very powerful, very toxic medicines to try to reverse the sick heart. The second thing you can do is put the paddles on a person's chest and give them a shock. Maybe you have seen this on TV. You can try to shock the shark teeth - that jagged rhythm - out of their heart.

I walk into the room. Lying on the hospital bed, there is this elderly gentleman who has known better days. He has been in and out of the hospital for the past month. His kidneys are gone. His lungs are shot. And now his heart is quivering. Shark teeth. About to bite into his life and take him away.

There is no pulse. There is no IV access. There is no way to administer any powerful medicines. This is a bad thing. My own heart is starting to go into V-tach.

The third thing almost never works. I have never, ever seen this work. But I did the third treatment for V-tach. *BOOM!* I thumped him in the chest. Not too hard, but just enough to know that I meant business.

Lub-dub, lub-dub, lub-dub, lub-dub. The shark teeth - the jagged rhythm - of his heartbeat were thumped out of his heart. His rhythm returned to normal, perfectly normal.

I place an IV in his neck, and we proceeded to give him some medicine to prevent the V-tach from recurring.

I have never seen this work before. Usually what happens is that the patient needs to be shocked and receive chest compressions. Most of the time, the patient dies. This gentleman did not die. His heart revived. He lived. He lives.

It got me to thinking. In order to change our heart, we must receive a shock, or a thump, or a dollop, or a whack. For a person to change their heart, something must overwhelm their conduction system. Something must overwhelm the poisoned heart rhythm in order to restart the heart in a new rhythm. I am talking about spiritual stuff now. No more ICU. I am talking about me and you.

If our spiritual center - our spiritual heart - is too scarred down by hatred, by anger, by pettiness, by guilt, by depression, by anxiety, then we are in danger of spiritual death. Some of us have experienced the spiritual version of V-tach. Our hearts are in a bad rhythm. If our hearts do not change, then we shall die.

I believe this is what Jesus was talking about. "Those who love me will keep my word, and my Father will love them. We will come to them and make our home with them. Whoever does not love me does not keep my words." These words come from Jesus' final sermon to his disciples.

Even though Jesus would die on the cross, some hearts would be closed to God. Even though Jesus would come back from the dead to teach and to heal, some hearts would be closed to God.

What is your spiritual rhythm? Is your heart in a good, strong steady rhythm? Is your spiritual heart in V-tach?

Are you ready to let Jesus shock you out of your poisoned rhythm? Are you ready to let God change your heart? "Those who love me will keep my word, and my Father will love them. We will come to them and make our home with them. Whoever does not love me does not keep my words."

I have another story. This is faith fable that my Dad shared with me. I do not know from where this story originated. A man was sleeping at night in his cabin when suddenly his room filled with light, and God appeared. The Lord told the man he had work for Him to do, and showed him a large rock in front of his cabin. The Lord explained that the man was to push against the rock with all his might. So, this man did, day after day. For many years he toiled from sun up until sun down; his shoulders set squarely against the cold, massive surface of the unmoving rock, pushing with all of his might. Each night the man returned to his cabin sore and worn out, feeling that his whole day had been spent in vain.

Since the man was showing discouragement, the Adversary – Satan - decided to enter the picture by placing thoughts into his weary mind: "You have been pushing against that rock for a long time, and it hasn't moved." Thus, the man got the impression that the task was impossible and that he was a failure. He became discouraged and disheartened. "Why should I break my back over this?" he thought. "I'll just put in my time, giving just the minimum effort; and that will be good enough."

And that is what he planned to do, until one day he decided to make it a matter of prayer and take his troubled thoughts to the Lord. "Lord," he said, "I have labored long and hard in your service, putting all my strength to do that which you have asked. Yet, after all this time, I have not even budged that rock by half a millimeter. What is wrong? Why am I a failure?"

The Lord responded compassionately, "My friend, when I asked you to serve Me and you accepted, I told you that your task was to push against the rock with all of your strength, which you have done. You did not have to MOVE the rock. Your task was to PUSH the rock. And now you come to Me with your strength spent. You think that you have failed. But, is that really so?"

"Look at yourself. Your arms are strong and muscled, your back sinewy and brown, your hands are callused from constant pressure, your legs have become massive and hard. Through opposition you have grown much, and your abilities now surpass that which you used to have. Yet you haven't moved the rock. But your calling was to be obedient, to push, to exercise your faith and to trust in My wisdom. This you have done. My child, *I* will now move the rock."

God wants us to push. God will move the rock. When we exercise the faith that moves mountains, we must know that it is still God who moves mountains. God wants us to push, to be obedient, to be faithful, to be strong, steadfast, courageous, loving. God wants us to push.

When everything seems to go wrong . . . just P.U.S.H.!

When the job gets you down . . . just P.U.S.H.!

When people don't react the way you think they should . . . just P.U.S.H.!

When your money looks "gone" and the bills are due. . .just P.U.S.H!

When people just don't understand you . . . just P.U.S.H.!

P= Pray
U= Until
S= Something
H= Happens

Are you ready to open your heart to God? Are your ready to be shocked out of your spiritual V-tach? Are you ready to PUSH. Are you ready to be strong with God, to grow a strong heart. Are you ready to follow the will of God: to love, to forgive, to rejoice, to reach out, to laugh with holy laughter, to cry for the broken hearted, to embrace the lost?

"Peace I leave with you; my peace I give to you. I do not give to you as the world gives. Do not let your hearts be troubled, and do not let them be afraid."

This is the gospel, the Good News of God's love for you. Let us pray....

The Outstretched Hand

When he had entered, he said to them, "Why do you make a commotion and weep? The child is not dead but sleeping." And they laughed at him. Then he put them all outside, and took the child's father and mother and those who were with him, and went in where the child was. He took her by the hand and said to her, "Talitha cum," which means, "Little girl, get up!" And immediately the girl got up and began to walk about (she was twelve years of age). At this they were overcome with amazement. He strictly ordered them that no one should know this, and told them to give her something to eat.

~ MARK 5:39-43

Loving, Holy, Healing God, your Son Jesus out-stretched his hand and healed the sick, restored the grieving, raised up the broken-hearted. We come to be healed. That we might know your love, your hope, your healing. Use these words for your purpose. In Christ's name, Amen.

I want to talk about healing - real healing - of the body and the soul. I want to talk about the story we just heard, and a bit about healing in the Christian tradition. But before all that, I want to talk about

I need to explain something. I am a doctor. I believe in my heart that modern medicine is good. Little children do not die from leukemia like they did 20 years ago. If you have a heart attack you have hope, real hope, that you will get better. If you have asthma, there are medicines that can help you breathe better. There are scans that can detect the smallest of tumors. Modern medicine has made HIV a chronic disease rather than a death sentence.

There is hope in modern medicine. There is power. There is real healing. I am a doctor. I believe that modern medicine is good.

Also, I think modern medicine can be invasive and dehumanizing. All those scans and blood tests and follow-ups. The strange language and fancy words. What are those doctors talking about anyway? I don't feel quite like a person when they are poking my belly.

At the same time, I recognize that the healing of the disease and the healing of the person is different. You can take the appendix out, but you still have the scar. You remember the pain. You remember the fear. Healing of the disease and healing of the person are different.

Now medicine is based on science. You have a theory; you have to do a test to prove your theory. But how do you prove faith? How do you scientifically prove God's power? Is it blasphemy to even try? Well, surprisingly, there are studies that show that prayer makes a difference in people's lives. People admitted to the coronary care unit were prayed for by a church group. Those that were prayed for had less complications. An infertility study out of Columbia University showed that those women who were prayed for had improved rates of pregnancy. There aren't that many studies, but there are enough to give even the most left-brained, scientifically-oriented, atheistic person pause. What is going on?

The other aspect of my background is that I was raised a mainline protestant. I grew up in a very traditional, wealthy, Calvinist church. The idea of a free-wheeling church service was to have hand-bells and a violinist. To have a healing service was just not in the spiritual landscape of my religious tradition. To have a healing service is not part of my intellectual tradition as a physician.

Yet, I must tell you that I believe the stories in the bible. I believe that the blind were made to see. I believe that the lepers were cleansed. I believe that the hungry were fed. I believe that the dead were raised. I share all of this personal stuff because maybe you and I are in the same place. Maybe you've never been to a healing service. Maybe no one has ever anointed you with oil or laid hands on you.

Maybe you and I are alike - people of a modern, scientific age, who are irresistibly drawn to the power and the mystery and the truth of Christ's healing hands.

The stories are many: a man possessed by demons prowls the tomb-stones. Jesus cleanses him of the demons and sends the demons into a herd of pigs to drown. Ten are healed of leprosy, and only one returns to give thanks to Jesus.

Lazarus is dead for four days. "There is the stench already," say his sisters. Yet, Jesus cries out, "Lazarus, get up!" And Lazarus gets up from the grave.

And then there is the final story of healing. The stone rolled back and Christ was alive. Christ was alive. Jesus was physically broken, even to death, but returned to be among the living. Brokenness is not the last word for Jesus, nor is it for those who follow Jesus.

And then there is this story: the crush of human suffering is upon Jesus. The crowds have swamped him. "My little girl is dying. Come," says the temple leader.

Before Jesus can make his way through the crowds, he feels something. A tugging, but something more, something just happened.

"Who touched my clothes?" Jesus turns around. It is a woman. She looks very pale, anemic, tired, weak, but she is smiling. She has bled for

12 years. She is relegated to the back room of her home. She is probably unable to marry. As the scripture says, "She had been under the care of many doctors and had spent all she had, yet instead of getting better she grew worse." We've been saying that for 2,000 years. "She has been under the care of many doctors, but she grew worse."

"Daughter, your faith has healed you. Go in peace and be freed from your suffering."

Jesus arrives. The little girl has just died. Jesus and three of his disciples hurry to the little girl's home. "She is not dead," Jesus says. "Only sleeping."

Jesus takes her by the hand and says, "Talitha koum!" "Little girl, get up!" Immediately the girl stands up, alive.

Amidst it all, with the press of the crowds, the hurrying here and there, Jesus says something that is our gift for today. When the temple ruler is anxious, hovering over him, Jesus says to him, "Do not be afraid, believe."

"Do not be afraid, believe." "Do not be afraid, believe."

And so here we are, you and I, the church. The world begins to rip off the scab of grief around September 11th. Many of us have been in and out of the hospital with physical illness. Many of us wrestle with struggles inside: depression, guilt, drugs, joblessness, homelessness, a bum relationship, a suffocating loneliness.

But because we are modern people, too strong, too rational, too independent, we miss out, and we do not ask God for help. We do not ask God for healing.

And so here we are. It is time to ask God to heal us. Heal us in our bodies. Heal us of our souls. Heal us of the demons that live in our minds. Heal us. It is time to ask God to heal our world - the anguish, the violence, the poverty, the injustice.

"Do not be afraid. Believe. Do not be afraid. Believe."

We are people of a loving God who wants to heal us. Christ came to walk with us and be with us. Christ waits for us to ask him. When we do ask Christ for healing, Christ will answer us. Not always in the way ask or expect, but Christ answers us.

Our healing service is not a medicine. It is not a quick fix. It is not a miracle. We simply ask God to do what God does. We invite God into our lives in a new way, to work his power, to work his healing.

"Do not be afraid. Believe. Do not be afraid. Believe." This is the good news. This is the promise of the Gospel. Amen.

The Bone of Luz

"Yet whatever gains I had, these I have come to regard as loss because of Christ. 8 More than that, I regard everything as loss because of the surpassing value of knowing Christ Jesus my Lord. For his sake I have suffered the loss of all things, and I regard them as rubbish, in order that I may gain Christ 9 and be found in him, not having a righteousness of my own that comes from the law, but one that comes through faith in Christ, the righteousness from God based on faith."

~ PHILIPPIANS 3:7-9

First, I want to give a lesson in anatomy. Then, I want to talk about Paul. And then, you, me, and the church.

First, the anatomy lesson. Do you know what the Bone of Luz is? Do you know what the Bone of Luz does? Now, I took anatomy class in medical school, and I had never heard of this bone until recently. I had no idea where this bone was in the body until recently. For thousands of years, physicians did not learn anatomy by examining the human body. Physicians learned anatomy from medical textbooks and lectures.

About 100 years after Jesus died, there was a great physician named Galen. Galen pulled together all of the medical texts of the great Greek philosophers and physicians - Hippocrates, Aristotle, Plato. Those guys never examined a human body either. Galen pulled together those texts and wrote a new medical textbook that became the standard medical textbook for the next 1,200 years. His word was medical truth, scientific fact, for 1,200 years. And Galen's text was based on writings that were more than 400 years old. And no one, because of taboo and social reasons, had ever examined a cadaver.

So, what is the Bone of Luz? The Bone of Luz is a bone in one of your toes that has the power to regenerate your entire body. For hundreds of years, scientists and doctors believed that there was a bone in your foot from which you could be entirely re-grown, completely resurrected, from your big toe. Scientific fact. Absolute truth. Not to be doubted for more than 1,000 years.

Now, what on earth am I talking about? Why am I talking about the Bone of Luz? What does this have to do with church? With my life? With my faith? Well, I will tell you! There are several lessons from the Bone of Luz. First, those scientists and doctors did not think, did not examine their patients, did not examine their own bodies, did not reflect on their experience. They accepted the doctrine of their trade as absolute truth, not to be questioned.

Second, scientific truth will always change. The rules of society will always change. The rules of government, the truth in medicine will always change. In my sort experience, the treatment for very common things: congestive heart failure, menopause, HIV, have been completely re-thought, re-made. This is good. When we think, we learn. When we learn, we grow.

When we think and pray and hope, we can learn more about God whose truth never changes. When we seek him with an open heart, we can understand better who God truly is. When we accept blindly, we get stuck, waiting for the Bone of Luz, rather than Jesus the Christ.

I want to change gears. Remember the Bone of Luz and the need to think and reflect. I want to talk about Paul. Paul's letters account for about two-thirds of the New Testament. Yet, Paul was not one of the 12 original disciples. He was from the other side. He was a Pharisee, a temple leader. He gives us his resume. "If anyone else has reason to be confident in the flesh, I have more: circumcised on the eighth day, a member of the people of Israel, of the tribe of Benjamin, a Hebrew born of Hebrews; as to the law, a Temple Leader; as to zeal, a persecutor of the church; as to righteousness under the law, blameless."

More than that, he was a Roman citizen. Most in Israel could not vote in the affairs of the Roman Government. What he is saying is that, "I have met every requirement to be at the top of society. I have the perfect credentials – a degree from an Ivy League university. I have a large house in the Hamptons. I sit on the Board of Directors of the Library, the Symphony, and several corporations. I drive a large Mercedes that floats me through my life."

Then, Paul says this, "Whatever gains I had, these I have come to regard as loss because of Christ. More than that, I regard everything as loss because of the surpassing value of knowing Jesus Christ my Lord. For his sake, I have suffered the loss of all things, and I regard them as rubbish, in order that I may gain Christ, and be found in him." (Philippians 3:7-8)

Paul reflected upon his life and realized that all of it was a myth, rubbish, a lie. The board of directors, the temple leadership, the house on the water, the Roman citizenship, the fancy degrees, the prestigious job, the high social standing, the (gasp!) Mercedes were all rubbish. All of it prevented him from seeing who he truly was: a child of God, a child of the resurrection, a person of the new way.

He had cast away the Bone of Luz - the myth of all those rules that always change - and embraced Christ the Messiah - the one who is steadfast, unchanging, all-knowing, ever-loving.

So, what about you? What about me? The church? If you believe that your resurrection will come from the Bone of Luz, you are mistaken. If you believe that meaning in your life will come from your social standing, from your possessions, from the positions you hold, you are mistaken. All of those things, unto themselves, prevent us from seeing who we truly are. Paul discovered that.

He was a rich man of prestigious social standing. He gave it all up to follow a carpenter from the back hills of Galilee. At the same time, maybe you believe that you don't have a fancy social standing, or enough money, or a big enough house, or a fancy job. Maybe you don't drive a Mercedes. Maybe you don't look like a magazine cover model.

I think our society does a good job of making people feel that - if you are not on the top - you are very much at the bottom. I must say this: God is alive in you. Christ is alive in this church, in this vineyard. Christ is alive is us. Christ is the cornerstone of this place. We tend the vineyard, not for ourselves, but for God.

I believe that when we let go of ourselves, Christ fills us. When we reflect inwardly and honestly, God fills us and we begin to look upward and out. Like Paul said, "I press on toward the goal for the prize of the heavenly call of God in Christ Jesus." Let us press on. It is our call. It is our joy. Let us pray....

Do You Want To Be Made Well?

Now in Jerusalem by the Sheep Gate there is a pool, called in Hebrew Beth-zatha, which has five porticoes. In these lay many invalids—blind, lame, and paralyzed. One man was there who had been ill for thirty-eight years. When Jesus saw him lying there and knew that he had been there a long time, he said to him, "Do you want to be made well?" The sick man answered him, "Sir, I have no one to put me into the pool when the water is stirred up; and while I am making my way, someone else steps down ahead of me." Jesus said to him, "Stand up, take your mat and walk." At once the man was made well, and he took up his mat and began to walk.

~ JOHN 5:2-9

Loving and Holy God, You give us a vision of what will be – there will be a new nation where your glory will be our light, where the leaves of the trees are for the healing of the nations. Let this nation rule in our hearts. Let this place be real for us today, right now. May these words point us to this holy place, in Christ's name, Amen.

I want to talk about disease and visions. First, disease. The first question is, "Do you want to be made well?" I have found this story more and more intriguing the longer I have done medicine. "Do you want to be made well?"

As the story goes, Jesus visits Jerusalem and goes by the Sheep Gate. By this gate there is a pool called Bethesda. As the tradition goes with this place, every so often the pool will bubble up, and the first person who steps into the pool to wash shall be healed of whatever affliction they have. So, you can imagine that there are quite a number of desperate folks waiting, waiting, waiting for the pool to bubble up, ready, ready, ready to be the first to jump into the pool.

This place is like a holy waiting room to see the Great Physician, except that you are not sure you have an appointment and you do not want to miss it when your name is called.

Enter Jesus Christ, the Great Physician himself, who enters the waiting room. He sees the people stacked up around the pool: the people who are blind, who are paralyzed, who are crippled.

One man had been lying there for 38 years. 38 years! Jesus looks at him and asks, "Do you want to be made well?"

I am intrigued by the man's answer. He does not say, "Oh, yes Lord, for you are the Son of God, and can make it so."

He does not say, "Oh yes Lord, I need to get well so that I can serve you, or help my family, or do something good for the world."

Do you want to be made well. The man does not say such prosaic things as, "Oh please Lord, for I am just so desperate." Or, "Please heal me for I am sick and tired of being sick and tired. I just need to get out of this place!" The man does not say these things. When Jesus asks him, "Do you want to be made well?" the man does not answer, "Yes, yes I do want to be made well."

Instead, he says, "Sir, I have no one to put me into the pool when the water is stirred up; and while I am making my way, someone else steps down ahead of me."

Huh? What does that mean? I think he is really saying, "I don't even know if I want to be made well again. I am too tired to hope. No one else cares enough about me. I can't even imagine what it would be like to be made well."

Jesus Christ, the Great Physician, says, "Stand up, take up your mat, and walk." At once, the man stands up, picks up his mat, and walks away. We never hear from him again.

As a physician, I take care of a fair number of very sick people. Many of my patients have HIV. I take care of folks with Hepatitis C. And there are several folks with pretty advanced diabetes and other medical problems.

And on more than one occasion, after the diagnosis is made – diabetes, HIV, or whatever – on the very next visit, the person will bring me the paper work to get disability entitlements. When I ask, "How is it going with the medications," I often get, "Oh, I haven't started the medications yet." "How is it going with physical therapy." "Oh, I haven't started physical therapy yet." "Did you make it to the nutrition appointment, the cardiologist, the neurologist?" "No, I haven't made it yet to that appointment."

It makes me wonder, when this happens, if the person would rather just be sick. If the person would rather check out of life, hang out by the Bethesda Pool, and just become "a sick person," with no vision or hope of being healed. In a deep way, I wonder if it is easier to be sick than it is to get better.

I wonder too, if we reflect upon our own lives, in what ways have we given up? In what ways have we gotten sick, and then let ourselves be sick, and not work for healing. In what ways have you given up, laid on the side of the pool, bemoaning that no one will help you.

What about that bad relationship that you just have to get out of, but you just keep dragging your heals? What about that addiction that has claimed you? What about the guilt that you keep carrying around? Do you find it easier to be angry at your children than it is to work on reconciliation? Do you find it easier to carry a grudge against your neighbor – it was all their fault anyway – than try to make amends.

When Jesus Christ asks you, "Do you want to be made well?" In your heart of hearts, what do you say?

There is an old story about an old Hasidic Rabbi who asked, "Where does God dwell?" And his followers replied, "God is everywhere, of course." And the old Rabbi smiled and said, "God dwells wherever we let him in."

Do we let God in for our healing? Or do we shut God out?

The two stories we read act like a see-saw to each other, and here is why. The first story is about a man who couldn't even imagine being well, a man who has lost his vision. The second passage comes from a man who was given the ultimate vision, the ultimate revelation about the true ending of the world.

Now, as I mentioned before, when non-Christians here the word, "Armageddon" or "Apocalypse," they get afraid. Indeed, there is good reason to be afraid because John's vision about the end of the world is indeed frightening. There is fire and brimstone. There is judgment – the wolves being separated by the sheep. We see the pure power of God being revealed that even the angels cringe. The Apocalypse is awesome, and it is frightening, and it is good.

John writes, "I saw no temple in the city for its temple is the Lord God the Almighty and the Lamb." No need for temples or churches because the consummation of God has arrived. Christ dwells with us. The whole city is one big church.

And then there is no sun, for as John writes, "And the city has no need of sun or moon to shine on it, for the glory of God is its light and its lamp is the Lamb."

And there shall be fruit from the tree of life, and the fruit will be ready each month, and the leaves will be for the healing of the nations." The tree of life which we were forbidden to eat in the Garden of Eden, we are now free to eat. Indeed, the leaves shall be used for the healing of the nations.

This is an awesome vision. This is the vision of God's holy purpose in the world – to bring all of us together as a holy people.

So, the first story is about a man who has lost his vision, could not even imagine walking again, resigned to his fate. The second story is about a man who has received the ultimate vision, the ultimate view of the universe.

Where do you stand amidst these two extremes? I have a vision that our church can be like that holy city Jerusalem. I have a vision that all who come here will be greeted as true brothers and sisters, that they shall be nourished in the Spirit, and find their home and their hope and, indeed, their salvation here.

I have a vision that our church will be outreaching in small ways and in big ways. We do not exist to keep our doors open, but that we reach out to those who need Christ, and bring them to our doors.

I have a vision that the light of God will be the light of this Church. Is this awesome? Yes! Is it frightening? Yes! Are we on are way? Yes! Yes! Yes!

I have a vision that our church can be like that holy city Jerusalem. I say let us dream big and aim high, for God is on our side and has big dreams and big visions for us as a church, and big dreams and grand visions for your life as well.

"And there will be no more night...for the Lord God will be their light, and they will reign forever and ever." Amen.

A Weak Faith for a Strong God

"The kingdom of heaven is like treasure hidden in a field, which someone found and hid; then in his joy he goes and sells all that he has and buys that field. "Again, the kingdom of heaven is like a merchant in search of fine pearls; on finding one pearl of great value, he went and sold all that he had and bought it.

~ MATTHEW *13:44-46*

Loving God, we seek the treasure of your kingdom. We pray that you would work in these words and in our meditations that we might grow in our faith, discover the treasure of your kingdom anew. In Christ's name, Amen.

I want to talk about predestination, sin, and the kingdom of heaven... weighty topics indeed for a warm summer's day. But first I want to tell a story about baseball.

When I was a kid, maybe 10 years old or so, I played baseball. Now, this might be hard to imagine, but I was a bit of a pudgy kid, a little shorter than most of the other kids. But, I loved baseball as a kid – the tawny smell of the glove on your hand, that sweet sound of a ball connecting with the bat. Mostly I liked hanging out with my buddies. Because I wasn't the best player, I spent a lot of time in the outfield. I would stand there hoping against all hope that the ball would not fly in my direction.

As providence would reveal, on a hot day in July, in the Pee Wee League of Scotia NY, game day between the two teams, one sponsored by the local pizza restaurant, the other by the local car dealership. Third inning. The pitch. A big lanky kid takes a swing. The ball shoots like a comet into the sky. *Oh God....* Deep into right field.... *Oh God this isn't happening...* The pudgy right fielder starts to move - legs pumping up and down, mustering speed. Awkward knees collide together. The right fielder trips. The glove extends into space.

Although it was 30 years ago, I remember it all perfectly well. I hear the *oohh* of the crowd. I smell the sweet grass smooshed into my face. I look into my glove. There, I discover, I am holding a baseball.

This moment changed my life. Up until that time, I only *played* baseball, but I was not a real baseball player. I did not think I could really do it. I was *on* the team, but I did not feel like I was a *member* of the team. At the top of the inning, when I went out to right field, I was playing baseball. When I walked back to the dug-out with the baseball in my hand, I was a real baseball player.

What could this story have anything to do about predestination, sin, and the kingdom of heaven. I will tell you, but not yet.

In our scripture today, there are two seemingly contradictory doctrines. These two contradictory messages have caused a lot of division and controversy in the church and has been a stumbling block for new believers. Until we can figure this out for ourselves, we can never have a real authentic faith.

Here is the first doctrine from Romans 8, "We know that all things work together for good for those who love God, who are called according to his purpose. For those whom he foreknew he also predestined to be conformed to the image of his Son, in order that he might be the firstborn within a large family. And those whom he predestined he also called; and those whom he called he also justified; and those whom he justified he also glorified." (Rom 8:28-30)

This is the doctrine of predestation. This is the doctrine that says, "God is all-powerful and because of this God decides *in advance* who is going to heaven and going to hell. Nothing you can do can change this. You might try to fulfill all the rules. You might give to the poor. You might be nice to your in-laws. But, if God did not choose you, you are cooked."

This tradition affirms the sheer grace of God. Nothing can save me, except for a loving God. I stand before the cross and my response needs to be humility and gratitude for Christ's sacrifice on the cross. This is where we get Calvinism. This is the tradition of the Reformation. The puritan congregational church is the heir to this tradition.

The second doctrine opposes the idea of predestination. This doctrine basically says that you must work out your own salvation. You must decide. You must make a decision for Christ. Once you do make a decision for Christ, then you are saved. In the gospel, we hear evidence of this doctrine,

"The kingdom of heaven is like treasure hidden in a field, which someone found and hid; then in his joy he goes and sells all that he has and buys that field. Again, the kingdom of heaven is like a merchant in search of fine pearls; on finding one pearl of great value, he went and sold all that he had and bought it." (Matthew 13:44-46)

You choose the pearl. You buy the field. This is the Baptist tradition. This is the tradition of the altar call and adult baptism. You must decide where you stand. What I find so interesting about our history at South Church is that we are the merger of these two very different traditions. I think every Christian holds these two doctrines in tension.

Both doctrines have weaknesses. On the predestation side, if God does all the work of my salvation, and it's all worked out ahead of time, then what is my role in my salvation? How do I know if I am saved or not? Why bother trying to do good deeds, it won't matter anyway.

On the free will side, if the decision for my salvation is completely up to me, if I decide for myself to be saved, what role does God play? God is completely out of the picture in my decision to be saved. Who is right?

There is a third very compelling position – the position of the secular world which says, "who cares?" There is no heaven or hell. There is no sin or salvation. There is only this world that I see; the world where the strong survive, where the powerful bleed the weak, and the poor can only suffer their lot before they die.

I want to propose a solution to this problem of predestination versus free will versus secularism. I came across this example from one of my favorite theologians and preachers, a guy named Tim Keller. The example is this: If I were falling off a cliff, and I saw a branch that I thought would save me, I would need to reach out and grab that branch. The branch is there, but I need to reach for it to know if I am saved. The branch is there – that's the predestination part. I need to reach for it to be saved – that's the free will part. If I never reach for the branch, if I doubt the existence of the branch, I perish – that's the secular part.

Here is the good part; I do not need to be absolutely, one hundred percent certain about the strength of the branch. A weak faith in a strong object is infinitely better than a strong faith in a weak object. The amazing thing about faith is that, what saves you is not the strength of your faith, but the strength of the branch. What saves you is not the strength of your faith, but God's strength to hold you.

Until I reach out for that branch, I will never know what it is like to be faithful. This is where the baseball story comes back. Until I really played, until I really tried, I never had that conversion experience to be, to really become, a baseball player. Like Paul said, "The Spirit helps us in our weakness; for we do not know how to pray as we ought, but that very Spirit intercedes with sighs too deep for words." (Romans 8:26) Until we reach out in our weakness, will the Spirit respond with God's strength?

As most of you know, in my role that complements my role at South Church, I teach resident physicians at Yale. These are folks who graduated from medical school and come from all across the country to Yale to do their specialty training. My job is to teach them, help them, become better doctors. I consider this an enormous privilege. The best part is not so much the teaching of the medicine, which anyone can learn about on google.com, but being a pastor to these young doctors.

Just about every single resident whom I work with, at some point in their training comes to me with doubts. "I don't think I can do this." "I don't think I'm smart enough." "I don't think I belong." My first reaction is, "You're crazy. I've read your file. I've looked at your board scores and your recommendations. You're smarter than I am, and I'm supposed to teach you."

I think this anxiety comes from the culture of modern medicine that says, "You have to be strong and smart, never tire, and above all you must always, always, always be right." If you are a physician-in-training, that is a set-up for failure. You are forced to have a strong faith in something that, at this point in training, is inherently weak – yourself.

Medicine is just the world I know. I am sure you have examples in your own profession – the culture of a law office, trying to bid on work for your landscaping business, surviving as a teacher. All of it has to do with being strong enough by yourself. The world is merciless with weakness, but in our faith, the Spirit helps us in our weakness; "for we do not know how to pray as we ought, but the Spirit intercedes with sighs too deep for words." (Romans 8:26)

It is infinitely better to have a weak faith in a something strong, than a strong faith in something weak.

What does this really mean for your life and my life? Right now in the pews, someone is thinking, "I could never really believe in all this. I could never be a Christian; because I just don't belong, or I don't know the Bible that well. Everyone else looks like *they* belong, but I just don't feel like *I* belong. I could never be a Christian."

That is simply not true. What saves you is not the strength of your faith, but the strength of God working in you. When that mustard seed takes root, the Spirit works in you. This is your destiny. This is who you are meant to become. At the same time, this is the work of your free will. If you can give your heart to this, God will change you and make you new. "For I am convinced that neither death, nor life, nor angels, nor rulers, nor things present, nor things to come, nor powers, nor height, nor depth, nor anything else in all creation, will be able to separate us from the love of God in Christ Jesus our Lord." (Romans 8:38-39) This is the promise of the Gospel. Amen.

Loving

The Audacity of Power

Thank you for this happy pleasure to address this weighty, vast topic: power.* I have been at Yale long enough to know that there are always lots of people smarter than I am, better read than I am. You know there are three stages to being at Yale. The first stage is that you feel like you don't belong because everyone else is smarter than you. The second stage is when you feel like you can hang in there with your colleagues. It's tough, but you belong here. The third stage is a mixture of the two: you feel like you belong but lots of people are smarter than you. And you are glad for that because your colleagues help make you a better person.

I realize that I am not as classy as a Dean Pellico or a Dean Angoff. I wish I were as cool as Jack Hughes, or as erudite as Thomas Duffy. I do not have that smooth August Fortonian way of communication. There are a lot of other people who are more qualified than I to give this talk about power. My main qualification is that I am a chief enthusiast for all of these projects – power day, doctor-patient communication workshops, professional responsibility. I spend my time waiting for the email to come, so I can be among the first to sign up.

You are all talented, brilliant students. You will be become talented, brilliant nurses, physicians, and PA's. But it is the stuff that we are about today – power, relationship, healing – that raises our field from a technical craft to an art. You are at a very special school indeed that gives its time and talent to this side of medical education: being transparent about

---

* Keynote Address to Yale medical students to address issues of power in medicine, October 2nd 2013.

power, raising up the importance of doctor-patient communication, delving into the complexities of professional responsibility.

BOLLYWOOD AND BAPTISTS

I asked a dear friend of mine, of my former residents, if I could tell her story. It is about power, but it is about more than power. This is her story.

Her name is Rita. It is the very first day of college – Pennsylvania State University. His name is Steven. There they all are – a bunch of 18 year old kids, first time away from home, college orientation. First day. They congregate on a rooftop to watch the sun set, to watch the sun set on their old lives. Rita and Steven meet. They talk. Steven notices that Rita is very cute. Rita finds Steven quite handsome. They talk some more. Their conversation wanders long into the night into the next morning. At this point, the data is unclear if there was any kanoodling on that rooftop.

The years roll by. They become good friends, something more than friends. They both land in Philadelphia for medical school. There is romance. Their relationship survives medical school. Things are getting serious. Steve applies in Optho and matches in Philadelphia. Rita applies in med-peds and matches in New Haven. What to do?

Here is the thing: Rita is actually Ritapurna Das. She is Bengali, a Hindu, the daughter of immigrants. When she goes "home" to visit her family, she goes to Calcutta. All of her family is Hindu. The person she would marry would, of course, be a Hindu. Honestly, no one really thought that much about it – it was just tradition and culture and family. All of that stuff.

Steven is Steven Fung, Chinese, more than that, a Baptist Christian. His families also are immigrants. Within America, they are an ethnic minority. Within China, as Christians, they are also a minority – a minority group within a minority group. For their son to marry anyone other than a Chinese Baptist is almost to defy imagination.

For Steven and Rita, their relationship was not so much a secret, but something private, just for themselves. Their parents maybe knew there was something happening, but it wasn't really talked about. So there they are. Steven in Philadelphia. Rita in New Haven. Slamming out 80, 90, 100 hours per week. What to do?

The moment of revelation came in the form of a hurricane. As fate would have it, they both have the same golden weekend. A golden weekend. Two days off. Together. Steven heads out on I-95 to race the hurricane that is plowing its way up the New Jersey coast. He loses the race. There is Steven, stuck in the 7th circle of hell on the New Jersey Turnpike, in bumper-to-bumper traffic in the middle of hurricane. There is Rita, worried about her fella. Eventually, he limps into New Haven, a soggy mess. They have the same revelation. "This is crazy. We love each other. We have to get married."

But what to do about the parents? Tender, delicate conversations ensue between child and parent. They love their parents. They go slowly. Their parents love their children. And so they listen. They seek to understand, because true love always seeks understanding. And they let it be. They let it go. For love always recognizes love. And then, they plan the wedding.

As a minister, I have never officiated in a Bengali-Chinese-Christian-Hindu wedding. In fact, I have never been to a Bengali-Chinese-Christian-Hindu wedding. In a word, it is awesome. It is a blowout. What a wedding. There is a Hindu ceremony led by a Hindu priest. There is a Christian ceremony led by yours truly. The bride and groom had four costume changes; and I had two. Drums. Processions. Ancient traditions. Holy Scripture from two traditions spoken in three languages. There is no wedding rehearsal: it's too complicated. You show up, march when the maître d' tells you to. When someone asks you a question, you say, "I do." Pow! Congratulations! You are now married.

My happiest moments as a Yale faculty member have been the occasions where I have married off residents and students. At great risk to my ordination status, I was among the first ministers in town to marry gay couples – in part because one of my residents was gay. In the hospital, you meet people who are different from you. And yet, we have this intense, shared purpose to care for the sick. And so, of course you fall in love with someone different from you. Most weddings I celebrate these days seem to be cross-cultural or inter-religious in some way. Love recognizes love.

The best part of the wedding was at the reception. The music at the reception played a lot of Indian Bollywood show tunes. I danced moves I never even knew that I had. But the best part of the reception was watching both sets of parents – especially Steven's parents, the traditional Chinese Baptists. They totally boogied down to the Indian Bollywood show tunes, right next to the Rita's parents. My guess is that they danced moves they never knew they had. And that is the story of how the Das-Fung family was born.

I asked Rita is I could tell their story. A love story on power day, why? There is the obvious: "baby, love is power." But there is a lot more going on. They had to figure out the truth and have the audacity to live out that truth. They had to navigate their cultural heritage, never compromising who they were, but building something new. To be true to themselves took courage, took wisdom, took power.

BURNOUT
As a residency program director, I am really interested in personal power, the stuff that is inside of us that keeps us upright. You all know how

hard it is to be on the wards. Well, I think you all know that it gets harder when you go to residency. You have likely had the experience of working with a resident who is on fire, who loves what they do, seems to enjoy patients, loves to teach, works well with nurses. At the same time, I'm sure you've had the experience of working with a resident whose hope seems to have collapsed, who has gotten crispy and burned out by the grind of it all.

I wanted to study this. Burnout. Who gets burned out. Who does not get burned out. And so we did. Myself and two other program directors — Donna Windish and Chuck Seelig — gave the medicine residents a survey. We asked every question we could think of. We asked about mentors, outside activities, time spent with family and friends, exercise, extra curricular activities, research involvement. I was really pulling for mentors. As a program director, if mentors were a strong variable, I could ramp up our mentor program. I also thought that maybe people who had a strong interest outside of the hospital or maybe an outside research project, some passion that got our gang revved up. Maybe that would make a difference in burnout.

Do you know what behavior made a difference in burnout in our study? NOTHING! Mentors, outside interests, exercise, friends, none of it made any difference in a residents burnout score. Bummer.

Interestingly, we asked a whole bunch of other questions as well. We asked about emotional coping strategies — denial, humor, venting, acceptance, and proactive planning. We asked about spiritual attitudes. There were two very strong predictors that correlated against burnout, that seemed to have some protective effect against burnout. I wasn't surprised at the first, but I was very surprised by the second. The two strongest variables that seemed to protect against burnout: gratitude and humility.

Gratitude I understand. There are people who have a stubborn gratitude. They score highly on questions like, "I am thankful for all that has happened to me." These are the folks who also enjoy their job and enjoy their patients more. That makes sense to me.

But humility was a surprise. Statements like, "When I wrong someone, I make an effort to apologize." "When I am ashamed of something I have done, I tell someone about it." This idea of reconciliation, of seeking forgiveness, goes against the tough Dr. House model of physician. And yet, right now, the happiest residents on the wards, the residents who have the highest satisfaction in their job, are the ones who live out this gift of humility and reconciliation.

Gratitude, I understand. The power of humility. I'm not done thinking about that yet.

GOOD NEWS
I have good news and bad news. Here is the good news: I read somewhere that 85% of everything gets better on its own. 85% of everything that your patients have will get better on their own. That weird rash. That upset stomach. "Doctor why am I so tired all the time."

Here is the bad news: 85% of everything gets better on its own. Without any intervention. For the most part, the body wants to heal itself, and our job is not to screw that up too much.

For the remaining 15%, most of the time we can help. We can take out the appendix, set the fracture, deliver the baby, chose the HIV meds, administer vaccines, and on and on. We can do a lot. This skill, this gift, is powerful stuff. Medicine is power. The audacity of it all, that with our pills and potions and scalpels we can actually do something to help. There is something medieval or mystical or Merlin-esque about this - that we have the power to make a difference in this way.

But the right pill or potion is not where our real power lies. 85%. 15%. It can be very difficult to figure out where our patient fits. 100% of the time our patients come to us for healing and for hope. And there is where our real power lies.

Sometimes medicine – the rush to fix things - gets in the way of real healing. The labs, the white coat, the sterile setting, the formality, the hierarchy, the paperwork, the business side of things, the billing forms, the regulations. Medicine can get between our patients and us. Our patients expect us to fix them, to stop their suffering. We are too often quick to prescribe a pill, when what our patients need is not Prozac, but hope. It is so easy to collapse into cynicism, to use power for your own gain, to simply give up.

I have been a minister for 22 years. That seems a crazy long time. I have only served urban congregations in some pretty rough neighborhoods where keeping oil in the boiler was an exercise in faith every month. I entitled these thoughts, "The Audacity of Power," as a transparent reference to Barak Obama's book, "The Audacity of Hope." I believe that hope really is a kind of power. To live with power and with hope is an audacious way to live indeed.

I learned early on that I cannot solve hardly any of the challenges my parishioners had. But I learned that I can commit. I can show up. I can hope. I can seek forgiveness. I can practice gratitude. In these tough neighborhoods, there are these communities of life and power and joy that are transforming lives and revitalizing neighborhoods.

Here is what am I trying to say: If you find yourself trapped on the New Jersey Turnpike in the middle of a hurricane, something really, really important is probably happening to you. You already have the power that you need to heal in this world. You can commit yourself to the truth that lies within. You can practice gratitude and exercise forgiveness. You can commit. You can hope. I believe this will forever endear you to your patients and lead to your own happiness in your art.

What you all are going through is very hard. Maybe you feel like you are stuck on the New Jersey Turnpike waiting for truth to reveal itself. But what I believe is that you have already arrived. Right now is your Bengali-Chinese-Bollywood blowout moment of revelation where it all comes together. I wish you the very, very best.

Eyes For Salvation, A Heart For Change

Now there was a man in Jerusalem whose name was Simeon; this man was righteous and devout, looking forward to the consolation of Israel, and the Holy Spirit rested on him. It had been revealed to him by the Holy Spirit that he would not see death before he had seen the Lord's Messiah. Guided by the Spirit, Simeon came into the temple; and when the parents brought in the child Jesus, to do for him what was customary under the law, Simeon took him in his arms and praised God, saying, "Master, now you are dismissing your servant in peace, according to your word; for my eyes have seen your salvation, which you have prepared in the presence of all peoples, a light for revelation to the Gentiles and for glory to your people Israel."

~ LUKE *2:22-40*

Loving God, Living Christ, in this New Year, we come to the temple to find you, to recognize you anew. Make it so, in these words, in our hopes and prayers, that we would have eyes for your salvation, that our hearts would quicken in your presence, that we would discover you anew. In Christ's name we pray, Amen.

I lift up the baby and say, "Welcome to the world! Welcome!" The little boy has just been born. He has no name yet. He is snuggled up in swaddling cloth with the blue and pink border that is in every hospital. Ears scrunched, and head a little lumpy from the delivery. Eyes closed. Easing in to this strange world. Still sleeping as they usually are when first born.

And there is that happy baby smell, that powdery, soapy, springtime baby smell. "All is calm. All is bright," just like the old hymn goes. "Welcome to the world! Welcome!"

There is much sweetness to it all, but there are some things that are at odds. The baby is too skinny; and the skin is thin, and feels a bit like paper. The baby was born 7 weeks early, and did not have those last few weeks to lay down some of that newborn chubbiness. Because the child is born early, the baby is in the Newborn Intensive Care Unit.

The eyes slowly open, as if to say, "Who is this strange man examining me?" As I say to all the babies, "I am Dr. Doolittle. I am your doctor. Welcome to the world!" There are two more things that give this baby a rocky start in the world. The mother is nowhere to be found. For reasons only she knows, she left the hospital suddenly. The baby is now a ward of the state, an orphan. There is one more thing. On routine labs, it was discovered that the mother is infected with HIV. For the kids, HIV is a very serious, life-threatening infection, but an infection that can be controlled with medications. With almost no prenatal care, this young baby is at risk of contracting the virus for himself.

And that is why I am this baby's doctor. I have a really unusual medical practice. In academic medicine, I have had the chance to fill in the gaps where there was need. I am trained in internal medicine and pediatrics - a double major of sorts. I work a bit in the Emergency Room. I take care of a lot of folks with HIV and Hepatitis C and narcotic addiction. I am faculty at Yale, but the clinic I run is in Waterbury - an outpost of sorts for Yale. When no one was caring these special babies in Waterbury, I stepped in.

"I am Dr. Doolittle. I am your doctor. Welcome to the world!" The Newborn Intensive Care Unit is a bubble of calm for what I fear awaits this young, nameless orphan, "Son of God, love's pure light." We start the

AZT. We give three doses of neviripine. We draw the labs. And then we hope. For that is all there is to do.

He was discharged in the care of a foster mom. They both came to the office this past Wednesday. The little baby now has a name, which given the circumstances should remain confidential. The baby is starting to get chubby. And then I learned maybe the happiest thing ever. The foster mom is *not* the foster mom. The foster mom is the *adoptive* mom. "I couldn't have children of my own," she tells me. "When I heard about this little guy, my heart went out to him... I knew that he was meant for me. Whatever the future holds, he will be my son, and I will be his mother."

We check the first of four blood tests in the computer: negative. The first blood test shows that the virus did not stick. There are medications to take for a few more weeks and follow up blood work in the months ahead. Adoption paper work for mom to fill out. But there is hope. More than hope, there is potential. More than potential, there is joy. Real joy.

There is another baby who was welcomed by the world during desperate times, not an orphan, but one who would have a rocky, uncertain future. In many ways, the little baby in my arms and the little baby in Simeon's arms start at the very same place. Mary and Joseph bring Jesus to the temple. He is 8 days old. As is the tradition, Jesus is there for his naming ceremony and to be circumcised. "Welcome to the world."

There is an old man there named Simeon. Simeon had been given a promise by God that he would see the "consolation of Israel" before he died. The "consolation of Israel" was a common saying at the time to refer to the Messiah. Interestingly, it comes from the same word that means, "comforter." Simeon was waiting for the consolation, the comforter, of Israel.

Simeon is an urban, patient, devout Jew. He has no need, no political ambition, nothing to gain, by making the claim that he makes. Simeon sees the baby Jesus, picks the baby up, and says to God, "My eyes have seen your salvation which you have prepared in the presence of all people, a light for revelation to the Gentiles and for glory to your people Israel." (Luke 2:30-33) There is hope. More than hope, there is potential. More than potential, there is joy, real joy. "Welcome to the world."

There was Anna, an old woman, who spends her days fasting and praying in the temple. Like Simeon, she lives in Jerusalem. She is urban, experienced, devout. Like Simeon, she too has nothing to gain to make the claim she makes. She sees the baby Jesus and recognizes that this baby is the one who will make things right for the world.

Both Anna and Simeon were faithful, devout people, but they also wanted change. They wanted Israel, their home, to be different. They wanted their lives to be different. They were waiting for the consolation, the comfort, of Israel. Maybe it was their openness to change that allowed them to recognize the baby Jesus, whose entire ministry was to call people to change, to renewal.

An important claim we make in our Christian faith is that God becomes flesh and dwells among us. This is really unique among world religions. Our faith is not only concerned with the hereafter, but also the here-and-now. We pray for God's kingdom to fully come, but we manifest that kingdom when we live in love, invite our neighbors over for a Christmas dinner, tutor kids at Northend School, reach out to those in need. Love becomes flesh and dwells among us. We are a faith that is all about renewal, about change. We believe that we can die to our old self and become a new creation in Christ. Like Jesus says, "Your sorrow will be turned to joy." (John 16:20) This is a very powerful claim.

In my life in the hospital, I talk about religion, spirituality, and church a lot with doctors and patients and all that. One of my friends and colleagues, Greg Boris, and I have the practice of swapping CD's, books on tape, inspirational speakers, stuff like that. One day he gave me a pretty cheesy-looking goal-setting CD.

I popped in the CD while I drove to work. It was as cheesy as I thought. "Make a plan." "Stick with it." "Write your goals down." All that stuff. But, the speaker - an impossibly handsome guy named Tony Robbins - was upbeat and positive. And so I did it. Back in 2008, I had three goals. First, lose 30 pounds and live a healthier lifestyle. Second, it's a big hang up for me, but I needed to publish in peer-reviewed journals in my life as an academic. If I didn't do this, my life as Yale professor would be over, so I got to it. Third, and this was most important, I needed to deepen my spiritual life. Not that it was bad before, but there is so much to enjoy with church, with prayer, with scripture. I wanted to deepen my compassion, reinvigorate my spiritual life, feel connected to God in a real way.

Lots of things happened; and it all took a lot of time. For goal number one, I became an enthusiastic vegan, joined a winter tennis league, and started lifting weights at home. I'm still prone to nibbling on Christmas cookies, but I am in a different place than I was 3 years ago. For goal number two, I've since published several articles and have a better discipline around writing those sorts of dry scholarly papers. For goal number three, I was very intentional about learning centering prayer and Christian meditation, and even yoga. Cindy Parsons taught me how to do Qi Gong. Tracy VanRhy introduced me to the Divine Office.

I am not perfect. I backslide and struggle. I am prone to lethargy and long naps. But I am in a different place now than I was three years ago. In great part, because I thought intentionally about my life, about my goals. I wrote them down, made a plan, reviewed the goals, and chipped away things. I felt accountable to my list and my plan, and that took on an energy all it's own. I asked God to help me, for the job of change is too big to do it alone.

Interested in this, I found a study that showed that if you write down your goals, you are 50% more likely to reach them. If you share those written goals with another person, you are 80% more likely to reach them.

It's a special day when January 1st falls on a Sunday. January 1st - a day when the Christmas cookies are tossed out and the resolutions are made. We as a church will soon embark upon a really big resolution - a capital campaign to raise 750,000 dollars.

In preparing this worship service, I thought it would be helpful and good and even fun for all of us to think about our own goals, to be the change that we want to be in the world. Each of us has goals. Each of us is the Simeon hoping for change. Each of us is the Anna looking for renewal of the way things are. What kind of person do you want to be? What is it about your life that needs to change? Our faith is about the here-and-now. Incarnation. Love made flesh. What do you want your life to look like?

As George will explain in greater detail, as you come to the communion table, you will find paper and markers. Write down a goal. A word. A sentence. Even maybe just a symbol. Be specific. Make a commitment to yourself. Tell another person about your goal. Ask God to help you.

You will also find a piece of paper in the bulletin. Write your goal down for yourself on this piece of paper. Make a plan. Take it home with you and put it someplace where you will see it - the bathroom mirror, the refrigerator door, your wallet. Be the change that you want to be in the world.

There is a baby in the temple, the love of God made flesh, the light of revelation to the Gentiles, and the hope of God's people everywhere. There is hope. More than hope, there is potential. More than potential, there is joy, real joy. "Welcome to the world." Amen.

The Ultimate Outsider

Then Philip began to speak, and starting with this scripture, he proclaimed to him the good news about Jesus. As they were going along the road, they came to some water; and the eunuch said, "Look, here is water! What is to prevent me from being baptized?" He commanded the chariot to stop, and both of them, Philip and the eunuch, went down into the water, and Philip baptized him. When they came up out of the water, the Spirit of the Lord snatched Philip away; the eunuch saw him no more, and went on his way rejoicing.

~ Acts 8: 35–40

Loving and Wonderful God, Like the Ethiopian whose life changed forever when he encountered your Word. Use these words for your purposes, that these words might be your words, that you might deepen our faith. In Christ's name, Amen.

I would like to talk about pain, real pain. Then I want to talk about the ultimate insider who was the ultimate outsider. Then I want to talk about good wine. As many of you know, part of my duties entails me working in the Emergency Room of Griffin Hospital. I don't work there too much – usually a Saturday shift or an overnight here and there.

The Emergency Room is an interesting place in that, most of the time, there is really no medical emergency at all. Maybe one-half, maybe more, of the people who come, come out of their emotional pain, their psychic pain. The young man who comes in with chest pain after a cocaine binge because his girlfriend broke up with him. The mother of two, who wrestles with depression, is found by the police intoxicated, wandering the streets.

The middle-aged man with back pain and says, "Only brand name Percocet can help me doc.... And I lost my prescription at the store.... Can I have more Percocet?"

The woman slashes her wrist in jail. The first ER doc sutures her wounds. Back at the jail, she chews through the sutures in her wrists, and returns to the ER, clothing soaked and says, "I just couldn't help myself.... I just hurt so bad."

I am at the beginning of my career in medicine, but in my short time, it seems that these visits to the Emergency Room are on the rise. Something is broken. Something is not right. Maybe there is fear of Al Qaeda or a general uneasy feeling in the world. The economy has tanked and many have lost jobs. Maybe there is a melt-down in the family – there is no other place to turn but to a nameless, faceless Emergency Room.

My theory is that every person has a reservoir of pain, a burden of pain, in their lives. Every person. Some have more suffering. Some have less. But each person has some burden of pain.

Maybe it is the shame and embarrassment of losing your job. Maybe you broke the law a few years back and have never recovered your self-esteem. Maybe you have been the victim of violent crime – a beating or worse. Or, maybe you witnessed a violent act of a loved one.

That is your burden of pain. That is you reservoir of pain in which you can drown yourself, which can swallow you up. And so many come to the Emergency Room. The nurses and doctors – we draw labs, check the Chest X-ray, pump the stomach, call the Social Worker, and it never seems to be enough. It never seems to be enough, because it is not enough. A pill is not enough to heal the reservoir of pain. The emergency room is not the right place to go to restore one's broken heart. I have an idea of which physician can help you, and where you can go, but first I want to talk about the Ethiopian man in our scripture.

The full name of the book of Acts is "The Acts of the Apostles," and it tells the story of the emergence of the Church. The scared, frightened shepherds and fisherman have emerged as confident leaders of a new movement that will change the world.

This book tells the story of a man who is, at the same time, the ultimate insider and the ultimate outsider. The man comes from Ethiopia – a long way from Jerusalem. He has come all this way to worship the one God in the temple. He is a rich man with a very high ranking in the Ethiopian Government – he is the head banker – akin perhaps to Alan Greenspan. He is powerful, respected, and rich. He is the ultimate insider.

But, he is also the ultimate outsider. He is different from every other person he meets. He is a eunuch, which means that certain parts of his body have been removed so that he would never bear children. Usually they are removed against his will at a young age. The hormones in his body that make him male are missing, so over time, he begins to look different. His voice changes. He speaks at a higher pitch. His skin changes. He looks a little feminine. He is the ultimate insider, but at the same time he is the ultimate outsider. He has no family to call his own, no children, no wife. He is different.

I can imagine this man standing at a large party of dignitaries and diplomats and thinking to himself, "I am so different from everyone else here. I am so alone. I am so utterly, completely alone."

Because of this feeling, perhaps that is why he ventures thousands of miles to worship the God of the Jews, because the home-town religion does not embrace him as an equal. He can be a new person in Jerusalem.

Philip is there on the side of the road as the Ethiopian eunuch is heading home. The Spirit moves him to approach the Ethiopian. Philip discovers the man is reading aloud from the prophet Isaiah, "He was led like a sheep to the slaughter, and as a lamb before the shearer is silent, so he did not open his mouth. In his humiliation, he was deprived of justice. Who can speak of his descendants? For his life was taken from the earth."

The Ethiopian eunuch reads this because it sounds a lot like himself: something was taken from him, and now he can have no descendants, "his life," "his children," were taken from the earth in the operation he suffered.

The Ethiopian reads this and, perhaps sees himself in these words. Philip, an old fisherman, approaches the finely dressed Ethiopian and opens his mind about Jesus: Jesus, who was led to the slaughter and humiliated, yet lives and triumphs over all evil; Jesus, who reaches out to the outsiders and embraces them as true children of God; Jesus, who as the Son of God, is the ultimate insider. Yet, the world rejected him as the ultimate outsider. The Ethiopian eunuch is so moved, that he is baptized on the spot. Church tradition tells that he returned to Ethiopia and started the church there.

Maybe you feel like the ultimate outsider? Maybe you have a reservoir of pain that presses in on your chest and makes your heartsick? The Emergency Room is not the place to go, but I do know a church on East Pearl Street where you can go. Jesus Christ, the Great Physician is there who will heal you, embrace you, make you whole, and bring you in as a true child of God.

At the Last Supper Jesus gathered his disciples around the table and he said to them seven statements that began with "I am" – things like, "I am the bread of life," and "I am the light of the world." The last of these statements is the one we heard today, "I am the true vine." "I am the true vine and my Father is the Gardener.... Remain in me, and I will remain in you. No branch can bear fruit by itself; it must remain in the vine. Neither can you bear fruit unless you remain in me. I am the vine; you are the branches. If a man remains in me and I in him, he will bear much fruit; apart from me, you can do nothing."

You are not an outsider. You are grafted to the life-giving vine of Jesus Christ. You are not an outsider. Christ has grown in you. You have grown in Christ. You belong to the vine that nurtures in you hope, warms you in the sunlight of holy love. You need not an ER physician, so much as you need the Gardener.

"I am the true vine and my Father is the Gardener.... Remain in me, and I will remain in you.... This is to my Father's glory, that you bear much fruit, showing yourselves to be my disciples." This is the good news. Amen.

Knowledge, Wisdom, Love

We know that "all of us possess knowledge." Knowledge puffs up, but love builds up. Anyone who claims to know something does not yet have the necessary knowledge; but anyone who loves God is known by him.

~ I Corinthians 8:1-3

Wonderful, Loving, Holy God, bless this time together, call out the unclean spirits, move in us with love and power. Bless these words, that they may be yours. In Christ's name, Amen.

I want to talk about knowledge, wisdom, and love. Each one of us has access to all the knowledge of the world. Each of us can walk into a public library and say, "I would like a copy of Moby Dick." If you want to know about angels, you go to the library or your browser and type in, www.angels.com.

Any medical article written in any of the hundreds of journals written in the last 40 years has been scanned into the computer. I go to the computer and Google some crazy thing like, "Wegner's Granulomatosis." And the computer will spit back 100,000 hits (I am prone to exaggerate, but this is no exaggeration!).

In a few seconds, you can discover when the high tide is in Hong Kong, the price of a latte in Paris, and the mating habits of the Emperor Penguin. This is knowledge. These are facts that you can learn. All the knowledge of the world is at your fingertips. And for the most part, this is a good thing. When you are at the hospital, and your doctor needs to check some drug-drug interactions, all she needs to do is take out her hand held device, push a few buttons, and bingo, there it is. This is good. We like this. Knowledge is good.

Yet, I believe in our world, in the 21st century, we place undue importance on knowledge. If you have missed the Internet revolution, do not despair. If you still use those...what are those things with the paper with the words written on them.... oh yes, books! If you still use them, do not worry. Having all the facts of the universe within easy access does not necessarily make your life easier. Knowing when the high tide of Hong Kong is does not make your life better. If you life feels empty, it is not because your ignorance about the mating habits of the Emperor penguin.

This is what Paul was talking about: the difference between knowledge, wisdom, and love. In the temples of the Greek deities, food offerings would be made. Then, afterwards, the food would be eaten. Sort of an ancient version of the coffee hour. Worship first, and then eat. The coffee is on, so keep the sermon short.

The food that you ate was the food that was offered to the Greek idols. This was a problem for the early Greek Christians. If you ate food from the Greek temples, were you condoning the temple practices? If you participated in the temple affairs, were you dishonoring Jesus? If others identified you in the temple, did you offend the church?

The early church had two opinions about this. One camp said, "Of course you can't eat the temple food. If you eat the temple food, you dishonor God. You dishonor your church."

The other camp said, "Food will not bring us close to God. We are no worse off if we do eat meat, no better of if we do." (I Cor 8:8) "What's the big deal eating at the temple? I worship the true God. The temple is just a statue, not a real God. I know what I believe. I know that my heart is with Jesus. Eating at the temple of the Greek idols is just that: eating at the temple, nothing more, nothing less. Everybody does it."

The first camp, says as a fore-runner to modern parenting techniques, "Just because everybody does it does not make it right." The second camp, "But my heart is right with God, with Christ, with my Church, what is the problem?"

Enter Paul. Enter a man trained in Hebrew law. Enter a man who knows how to play one law against another. Enter a man with knowledge – and also with wisdom. What Paul says is so artful, so clever, and so wise. Paul says, "Take care that this liberty of yours does not somehow become a stumbling block to the weak. For if others see you, who possess knowledge, eating in the temple of an idol, might they not, since their conscience is weak, be encouraged to the point of eating food sacrificed to idols? So, by your knowledge, those weak believers for whom Christ died are destroyed." (I Cor 8:10-11).

The difference between knowledge and wisdom is that knowledge is this: wisdom is knowing what to do with those facts. Wisdom is how the mind finds faith in the same way that love is how the heart finds faith. I will say that again because I believe it to be important. Wisdom is how the mind finds faith in the same way that love is how the heart finds faith.

An old church that grew out of the earliest reformation movements in Eastern Europe was the Moravian church. They have a wonderful statement of belief. Their creed is, "In essentials, unity. In non-essentials, liberty. In all things, charity."

Enter Jesus. Jesus did not have the training of Paul. He was raised a carpenter's son. Yet, when he taught in the temple, everyone said, "He teaches as if he has authority, and not as the scribes."

Jesus did not have the training of a scribe of a Pharisee, but he had wisdom. His was the mind of God. When the unclean spirit, who had possessed a man, saw Jesus, he recognized him. "What have you to do with us Jesus of Nazareth? Have you come to destroy us? I know who you are, the Holy One of God?" "Be silent, and come out of him," said Jesus. Jesus had love and power and faith.

I want you to have this knowledge: the Christ who cast out that unclean spirit is the Christ who protects and loves and leads you today. I want you to have this wisdom: let your mind and your heart shape your life to lead your home. Wisdom is how the mind finds faith in the same way that love is how the heart finds faith. Let us be mindful of that old Christian creed, "In essentials, unity. In non-essentials, liberty. In all things, charity." Let us pray....

The Leper Within Us

Elisha sent a messenger to him, saying, "Go, wash in the Jordan seven times, and your flesh shall be restored and you shall be clean." But Naaman became angry and went away, saying, "I thought that for me he would surely come out, and stand and call on the name of the Lord his God, and would wave his hand over the spot, and cure the leprosy! Are not Abana and Pharpar, the rivers of Damascus, better than all the waters of Israel? Could I not wash in them, and be clean?" He turned and went away in a rage. But his servants approached and said to him, "Father, if the prophet had commanded you to do something difficult, would you not have done it? How much more, when all he said to you was, 'Wash, and be clean'?" So he went down and immersed himself seven times in the Jordan, according to the word of the man of God; his flesh was restored like the flesh of a young boy, and he was clean.

~ II Kings 5:10-14

Loving God, we come for hope, for healing, for good news. Let your Spirit move in these words and our meditations. Bless this time together; give insight for our minds, courage for our heart, and strength to our faith. Bless these words that they would be Yours. In Christ's name, Amen.

I want to talk about Insiders and Outsiders, Leprosy, HIV, and about how all of this impacts your life and mine. The story of II Kings tells one of the most poignant healing stories in all the Hebrew Scripture, but there is a lot more going on then just a man being healed of leprosy. Insiders, Outsiders, Leprosy, HIV, you and me, here we go.

Insiders: General Naaman is the ultimate Insider. General Naaman is the leader of King Aram's armies. He stands on the right hand of the king when he enters the temple. He is the Insider's Insider, the right hand man of the King.

In this passage, the Insider is also the Outsider. Here is the general, the leader of all the armies, the trusted advisor to the King, who sits on his right hand. He is the ultimate insider, but he is also the ultimate outsider. General Naaman has a secret. General Naaman has a spot. General Naaman has leprosy.

As you will recall, leprosy in those times was viewed as a curse from God. People with leprosy were cast out of society, to live out their curse, separate from their communities. In those times, leprosy equaled expulsion, shame, and separation. General Naaman is complicated: the most powerful man in the kingdom next to the king with a common devastating, shameful affliction that devastates the lives of rich and poor alike.

I did not realize until I was a missionary in India some years back that leprosy still exists today. It is increasingly rare. Leprosy is caused by a bacteria – a cousin to tuberculosis- that infects the nerves. Leprosy does not eat away the tissues – it is more insidious than that. The infection kills the nerve, so that you lose you lose sensation in your hands, your feet, and your face. The nerve damage leads to problems in the blood supply. You lose your sense of touch. The smallest cut, a slight burn that you do not feel, leads to chronic, festering infections. It is the chronic infections and trauma that causes people with leprosy to lose their fingers and toes. But of course, folks did not know about mycobacterium back then. Back then, if you had leprosy you were being punished by God. You were a sinner.

General Naaman, the ultimate insider, the right hand man of the king. What does he do? He does what other insiders have done for centuries: he goes to another insider, the King of Israel. He does what insiders, power brokers, lobbyists, corporate titans still do today – he brings a ton of cash. He wants to strike a deal. I will give you cash, and you will heal me.

But, as everyone knew back then, there was no cure for leprosy. The King of Israel panics. The general of the most powerful army on their northern border expects to be healed. Cash for healing. "Does he think I'm God?" the Israeli King asks aloud. Elisha sends word to the King, "Send the General down my way, and we shall see what we can do."

Let us pause for a moment. Imagine that the Queen of England shows up in your driveway. The stretch limos, the Ford Explorers with tinted windows. You could go outside, greet the Queen – she is the Queen after all. Instead, you send out your five year old daughter, "What do you want?"

The same thing happens with Elisha and the General. The General arrives with a long parade of camels and horses, gold and silver, aids and guards, and on and on. Does Elisha go to the door? No. He sends a servant. "Go and wash seven times in the river Jordan," says the servant. Elisha does not bother to speak to the General directly.

The General thinks about the muddy, paltry Jordan River. "But there are better rivers back home," he says. He is irritated. "Long journey. Lots of cash. The prophet Elisha doesn't even see me. A servant tells me to wash in their muddy river."

But the servants say, "If he asked you to do some hard thing, you would have done it." And so, the General washes seven times in the Jordan River, and "his skin becomes clean like that of a young boy."

What is going on here? When General Naaman brings all that gold and silver to the prophet Elisha, he expects payback. He treats God just as he would any other foreign king or foe. If you can't beat 'em, buy him off; and God is yours.

We might think that we are too sophisticated for this. We do not try to manipulate God. But hold on a minute: I go to church every Sunday. I am nice to people. I try to be a good person. Doesn't God owe me? Won't God give me what I need? One more question: do you have faith in your cash more than you have faith in your God? General Naaman certainly did.

God is not a God of love if he expects payment before doing a good thing. God is not a God of power if God owes you when you pay up.

When General Naaman is told to wash in the river and that his money is no good here, he is stripped away of his power. He is stripped away of his title. He is stripped away of his prestige. He becomes a man, hurting and scared, naked in the muddy waters, hoping beyond all hope that he would be healed. Then, and only then, does he discover what it means to experience a God of love and power. Then, and only then, does he know a God of grace.

Let's talk about Outsiders. Who is the Outsider? The slave girl. We do not even know her name. She is a slave. She has no possessions. In fact, *she is* a possession. Her life and death are in the hands of the Queen. Her parents may be dead, likely not with her, of this we are not sure. But we know that she was the prize in a skirmish between Israel and Syria. She dwells in a foreign land, away from her home. She is the Outsider, the Slave, and the Servant.

But yet, surprisingly, amazingly, she is moved with compassion for her Master. She is the reason why General Naaman has any hope at all of getting cured. She is moved with – dare I say it? – *love* for the one who conquered her land. "If only my master would see the prophet who is in Samaria," she says. "He would cure him of his leprosy." (II Kings 5:3)

Why would the conquered slave offer this hope for healing? In her case, we can only speculate, but I know that when we are at our best as Christians, our mission, our very being, is to reach out to the outsiders. When we are at our best as Christians, we see only the hurting man in need of help and healing, because that is how Jesus sees you and me.

The General, the most powerful man in the kingdom, knew fear and would pay any price to fix it. The slave girl has nothing, but yet has the strength to forgive her captor and offer him the one thing he needs. She has a loving heart and the courage to speak up. In this marvelous story, who has the power? Who is the Outsider? Who is the real Insider?

Reflect for a minute on the ways that you are an Insider in this world. Do you have money? Do you have status? Are you "important" in your circle of friends or at work? Think about how being an insider might get in the way of standing in the mud of the Jordan River asking God for help.

Think about ways that you might be an outsider to society. Are you gay? Is English your second language? Do you have a chronic illness that makes life hard? Do you have a secret that you think is so terrible, so awful, that no one would ever think of you the same way if we knew about it?

We are a church with a great tradition of welcoming all people. Think about what people in this church did to welcome you when you were the Outsider. At one time in your life, we were all strangers, outsiders, to this place. Yet, here we are on a hot day in July worshipping God together. Something happened here to each of us where we felt a call to be here, that we belong with God here. Something happened to us where we felt like an insider, where we belonged. I would love to hear what that story was for you.

I believe that one measure of our strength-in-love is our ability to welcome the stranger, the Outsider. The slave girl had every reason to stab General Naaman in his sleep. Yet, she saw in him a man in need of healing.

My hunch is that many of us spend a great deal of time in our lives trying to be more like the General than the Servant. I admire the General in one respect: he was willing to take a risk. He was willing to venture into the land of his enemy in hope that his life would change. The General stepped out of his comfortable world of power and status to humble himself before a foreign king and a prophet with attitude. The General had hope. The General had faith that in a world of so much posturing and falsity, his servant girl might actually be right: there is a God who can heal me of my leprosy.

When he stepped out of the muddy Jordan River, his skin was clean, and he stepped into a new life of faith. He says to Elisha, "Now I know that there is no God in all the world except in Israel."

Jesus sent His disciples out in the world two-by-two with nothing but a staff and a cloak. He takes away their trappings so that they can walk by faith and not by sight.

I believe this is the faith that we need in our lives. The faith that changes us and makes us new. The faith that comes when we experience the God of power and grace that takes away the leprosy that is within me, the shame that is in me and you, the doubts, the worry. I believe we need this faith of the Outsider General who finds his true home.

We need the faith that gives us the courage to speak out in true love amidst the horror of a war in Iraq. We need the faith that gives us comfort amidst the suffering and loss of a family member. We need the faith that makes us bold to reach out to the stranger. We need the faith that gives us sure and certain hope that we are not adrift in this frenetic world, and that we belong to God.

Maybe this is why we come to church. The rest of the world, in our jobs, in the rhythm of our lives, wants us to be Generals, but really, in our heart of hearts, we want to be servants. We *need* to be servants. We want to stand in the mud and suffering of the world in sure and certain hope that we will be healed, that the world will be healed.

And so brothers and sisters, let this be our prayer, that this would be our faith. For the glory of God, Amen.

Christin the World

*He entered Jericho and was passing through it. A man
was there named Zacchaeus; he was a chief tax collector
and was rich. He was trying to see who Jesus was, but
on account of the crowd he could not, because he was
short in stature. So he ran ahead and climbed a sycamore
tree to see him, because he was going to pass that way.
When Jesus came to the place, he looked up and said to
him, "Zacchaeus, hurry and come down; for I must stay at
your house today." So he hurried down and was happy to
welcome him. All who saw it began to grumble and said,
"He has gone to be the guest of one who is a sinner."
Zacchaeus stood there and said to the Lord, "Look, half of
my possessions, Lord, I will give to the poor; and if I have
defrauded anyone of anything, I will pay back four times as
much." Then Jesus said to him, "Today salvation has come
to this house, because he too is a son of Abraham. For the
Son of Man came to seek out and to save the lost."*

~ LUKE 19:1-10

Loving, Holy God, Give us the ears to hear you. Give us the heart to
love you. Give us the heart to heed you. Bless these words and let
them be yours. In Christ's name, Amen.

We are Christians. We identify ourselves by His name. How are we to
be faithful Christians in the United States of America? How are we to
be Christ in this world? This can be a complicated question. Both our

presidential candidates have professed their Christian faith publicly in the debates and in the media. It has become in vogue and politically astute to be politely religious. We are a secular, pluralistic society. Yet, 90% believe in God in one Gallup study. And in another 42% identify themselves as being born again. We are secularly religious, or religiously secular, where it is culturally cool.

Today is Halloween, a secularization of All Saint's Day, which is tomorrow. Some preachers will bemoan this day as celebrating demons. But the tradition simply grew out of the belief that the evening before All Saint's Day was "Hallow'd" or "Holy."

I want to talk about Christ in the world, how to be a Christian in the world. The world is starved for God. Our country is starved for God. I believe there is an ache and a loneliness among our brothers and sisters, our neighbors.

Pop psychologists might call us the "self-esteem people." It is all about our "self-esteem." I need caps on my teeth and Botox to "build up my self-esteem." I want to meet new people and get promoted, and so I must "build up my self esteem." "He didn't mean to burn down his mother's house and rob the bank, he suffers from low self-esteem."

The concern I have about being the "self-esteem people," is that there is an emphasis on "self." This is a bastardization of Yankee Puritanism: pick yourself up to improve yourself. Find the power within. The Puritans get blamed for this self-reliance. But actually, the old Yankee spirituality emphasized an absolute reliance on the Providence of God.

The world is starved for God, and I would say it goes way beyond self-esteem. I think the challenges we face as a community are largely spiritual. There is a spiritual isolation, a sadness, a loneliness, as if we are a people that does not know our true home.

As I speak these words, I think about people who have come to me for their medical care. A man with HIV who financed his crack habit by prostituting himself. The 95 year old woman who shows up in the ER because she had a fight with her daughter. "Just admit me," she says. "My daughter always yells at me. She hates me so much." My heart goes in free fall at the thought of their suffering and struggle.

And on and on – the incredible crush of human suffering. It makes you want to curl up into a ball and take a nap until the second coming. "Page me when it's over." But checking out is not who we are called to be.

The answer, I believe, to our society's ills has everything to do with good health insurance, good jobs, opportunity, good schools. But more than that, I think we need, as a country, a change of heart. We throw money at our problems. We throw Prozac. We throw anger and self-righteousness at our problems. Our problems are earthy and real, but the solution – the more I realize this as a physician – really is spiritual.

I do not want to sound glib. But my patient who prostitutes himself has stopped because he has found a new sense of self. He needs a job, but he needs a new heart, and he is reaching for it. He realizes that his body is a temple, that he is made in the image of God, that he is special. As he comes to know this, he realizes that he simply cannot prostitute himself, for he is not for sale. God already owns him.

Friends, I realized that I have spoken about politics, prostitution, pop psychology, and Botox, but I put a question to you and want to share an answer. How are we to be Christ in the world? When I was a teenager, a wild-eyed lady approached me in the CVS, stared at me in the face, and implored me, "Are you saved? Accept Jesus and be saved?" Is that what we are supposed to do? I was not sure if she were nuts or a demon or had mistaken me for someone else.

Are we supposed to be like Chuck Ripka who is a mortgage broker and runs a Christian Bank? He prays with you over your loan application that you might get the best deal on a house.

This is how I believe we are to be in the world: transparent. I want to be transparent to Christ. That everything I say, everything I do reflects God's will in my life. That when I preach, my words are faithful. That when I meet a patient in my clinic, I could be compassionate the Jesus would be. That in my secret thoughts, they might be imbued with compassion and love for the world – even when that guy cuts me off in New Haven.

Should we follow the teaching of St. Francis of Assisi, "Preach the Gospel daily. Use words when necessary." Zacchaeus was a rascal. He was a tax collector, which meant that he worked on a commission basis for the Roman Government. You collect a certain amount, send it off to Rome, but then you had license to keep on collecting taxes to build a Jacuzzi in your living room. Zacchaeus was not a popular guy. He worked for the oppressive, occupying Roman force, and fleeced his neighbors for all they were worth. He was a man of the earth, making money, working the system.

He had money, but he had a whole in his heart. When he saw Jesus, he encountered God. He saw in Christ his true home, his hope, his life made whole. "Come to my home for dinner."

Unbelievably, to the grumbling of all the regulars, Jesus did dine with him. What did Jesus say to Zacchaeus to make him change his heart. God heals many people: "Get up off your mat and walk," "Bathe in the river Jordan and your leprosy will be healed," "I will rub this mud in your eye and you shall see," "Lazarus, get up."

"Zacchaeus, open your heart to me." Maybe that's all it took. For Jesus was the word made flesh. In his words, there was love and God's power. Transparency.

Paul wrote to the Thessalonians. "We must always give thanks to God for you, brothers and sisters, as it is right because your faith is growing abundantly, and the love of everyone of you for one another is increasing. To this end we always pray for you, asking that our God will make you worthy of his call and will fulfill by his power every good resolve and work of faith, to that the name of our Lord Jesus may be glorified in you, and you in him, according to the grace of our God and the Lord Jesus Christ."

We can do this. We can be like the church in Thessalonica. We can be so changed like Zacchaeus. We can be transparent to Christ. That we can be generous in our giving, open in our loving, visionary in our serving.

We can be transparent to Christ – alive in His Spirit, empowered in His Love, comforted in His Steadfast presence.

"Open your heart, Zacchaeus." "Open your heart, Ben Doolittle." "Open your heart, Eric." "Open your heart East Pearl." "Open your heart Vivian." "Open your heart, Donna." "Open your heart Shirley." "Open your heart Sara." God with us. The church – you and me – transparent to Christ. For his glory, for our salvation. This is the power of Christ. Amen.

Resurrection

Mary stood weeping outside the tomb. As she wept, she bent over to look into the tomb; and she saw two angels in white, sitting where the body of Jesus had been lying, one at the head and the other at the feet. They said to her, "Woman, why are you weeping?" She said to them, "They have taken away my Lord, and I do not know where they have laid him." When she had said this, she turned around and saw Jesus standing there, but she did not know that it was Jesus. Jesus said to her, "Woman, why are you weeping? Whom are you looking for?" Supposing him to be the gardener, she said to him, "Sir, if you have carried him away, tell me where you have laid him, and I will take him away." Jesus said to her, "Mary!" She turned and said to him in Hebrew, "Rabbouni!" (which means Teacher). Jesus said to her, "Do not hold on to me, because I have not yet ascended to the Father. But go to my brothers and say to them, 'I am ascending to my Father and your Father, to my God and your God.'"

~ JOHN 20:11-17

Loving God, Holy God, You sent your Son into the world so that whoever would believe in Him would have eternal life. Bless this gathering, God. Bless our meditations, our prayers, our being together. Bless these words, that they would encourage us to new life in you. In Christ's name, Amen.

Do not doubt the resurrection. Do not explain it away. Do not sit comfortable with this big thing. As you know, I work often as a physician in a local emergency room. There, I have seen resurrection. I have been the instrument of resurrection. I have cared for the 20 year old young man who poisons himself with heroin. He stops breathing. His heart stops. His compatriots drop him in the parking lot of the Emergency Room. Compression. Compression. Push. Push. Breathe. Breathe. Narcan IV. Stat. Pulse. Pulse. Blood pressure. Life. Life. Life. Resurrection.

I have seen the man keel over upon his arrival, collapse to the ground. Shock. Shock. Shock. Thump. Thump. Amio load. Breathe. Breathe. Life. Life. Resurrection.

I have seen life grow from death. But what a physician does is small. For the people who come back to me are not truly dead. They are nearly dead, nearly gone, close, but not quite. It is not magic. It is not a miracle. You follow a recipe, a list of options. But to watch a man come back to life like that is a privilege. It is grace. If you and I can do a small thing, God can do a great thing, a big thing.

Do not doubt the resurrection. Do not explain it away. Do not sit comfortable with this big thing.

Years after the resurrection, (but still 2000 years before the DaVinci Code and Mel Gibson's Passion of the Christ), Paul wrote to the fledging church in Rome, "If you confess with your lips that Jesus is Lord and believe in your hear that God raised him from the dead, you shall be saved. For one believes in the heart and so is justified, and one confesses with the mouth and so is saved." (Romans 10:8-13)

If you believe in the resurrection, if you believe that Jesus rose from the dead, then you are saved. But what does this mean exactly? On Easter Day, two things happen: either Easter becomes too religious or not religious enough.

"Pastor Ben, are you telling me not to get too religious?" Now, the tradition of the church if filled with powerful statements that have become platitudes – empty phrases. We hear from the TV evangelists – "Accept Jesus as your personal Savior", "Confess to Christ and be saved." I have a problem with those statements. Not because they are untrue, but because no one knows what they truly mean any more, for they are repeated so very often and heard so very often, almost like a mantra or a school song. That's what I mean by making Easter too religious – we use the language of the religion, but forget the truth behind the world.

On the one hand it is easy to turn the resurrection into a litany of empty phrases – to pay lip service to the resurrection. On the other hand, it is fashionable in the year 2004 to be cynical about religion, about faith, about Jesus. It is intellectually fashionable to say, "The resurrection is just a story." The church is a crutch for the weak.

In pleasant circles, it is socially acceptable to say things like, "I don't believe that Jesus actually rose from the dead, I believe it's more like a metaphor for the rebirth in all of us."

In these days, we need a Savior. We need Jesus. In these days, when the names of cities invoke images of violence – Fallujah, Madrid, Jerusalem, New York – we need salvation. We need to know who our Savior is.

Jesus Christ did not walk on the ground with us, heal the sick, and preach good news to the poor for us to pay lip service to Him, for us to explain him away because our hearts are too small to understand him.

"Accept Jesus Christ as your Savior and you shall be saved." Think about how you live your life and try that phrase on in a different way. How do you live your life? To whom do you turn for your salvation?

"Accept your job at Dunkin Donuts as your Savior, and you shall be saved." Salvation at Dunkin Donuts! That sounds just plain ridiculous. But how do you live your life?

"In the name of Yale University, and you shall be saved." While some may believe this, it is just plain ridiculous.

How do you live your life? To whom do you turn for your salvation? "Accept Jack Daniels as your Savior, and you shall be saved."

"In the name of *your own name*, you shall be saved." But of course, if you live for those things, you shall not be saved. You shall perish.

How do you live your life? Have you given your life over to something else – the grind of your job, the roll of the dice at Mohegan Sun. What do you live for? If you live for your job, you shall die for your job. If you live for the bottle, you shall die for the bottle. If you live

If you believe that Jesus Christ rose from the dead, if you believe this, what happens to you? How is it that you live differently?

If you believe that Jesus rose from the dead, then your mind is open to God's presence in your life.

If you believe that Jesus rose from the dead, then your faith is stronger than your guilt.

If you believe that Jesus rose from the dead, then your faith is stronger than your cynicism.

If you believe that Jesus rose from the dead, then your heart is open to the power of God.

If you believe that Jesus rose from the dead, then your mind is free – your mind is free from the confines of your small reality and open to the vastness of heaven.

If you believe in the resurrection, then you are free.

If you believe in this day, this resurrection, then your whole life changes. It changes in two ways. First, you live your life differently from everyone else around you. The rest of the world seeks validation from the world. The rest of the world is trying to get promoted, get in the paper, have the right friends, run with the beautiful crowd.

The world wants to be the self-assured, jaded, intellectual, literati, glitterati, rigatoni, and macaroni. People in the world want to be the big cheese.

But if you believe that Christ died for you, that Christ rose for you, then the need for the world's validation simply drops away. You no longer need to look to the world – your job, your friends, and your family – for your validation, for your salvation. You like those things, but you don't cling to them with the same desperation. Your joy is with your God.

The second thing that happens in your life is that you want to share this good news. You want to serve. You want to be like your Savior. You want to do what he did. You want to reach out to those in need. You want to love your neighbors – even those different from you. You want to eat better, think better, live better. You want to be like Jesus. Compelled by gratitude. Compelled by love. Compelled by joy. Resurrection. Resurrection. Resurrection. Let us pray....

The One Who Comes

In that region there were shepherds living in the fields, keeping watch over their flock by night. Then an angel of the Lord stood before them, and the glory of the Lord shone around them, and they were terrified. But the angel said to them, "Do not be afraid; for see—I am bringing you good news of great joy for all the people: to you is born this day in the city of David a Savior, who is the Messiah, the Lord. This will be a sign for you: you will find a child wrapped in bands of cloth and lying in a manger." And suddenly there was with the angel a multitude of the heavenly host, praising God and saying,

> *"Glory to God in the highest heaven,*
> *and on earth peace among those whom he favors!"*

When the angels had left them and gone into heaven, the shepherds said to one another, "Let us go now to Bethlehem and see this thing that has taken place, which the Lord has made known to us." So they went with haste and found Mary and Joseph, and the child lying in the manger. When they saw this, they made known what had been told them about this child; and all who heard it were amazed at what the shepherds told them.

~ Luke 2:8-18

Christmas is not about more. Christmas is about less. I want to share three stories about Advent, the season of expectation and waiting.

238

First, I need to share a story that has filled up my heart and filled up my mind with thought. I am working in the Emergency Room one night. An overnight shift. A rainy, rainy night. Darkness. A quite night, drinking coffee, surfing the web. Thank God for a quiet night.

Parents bring their two year old in. The two year old is smiling and happy, toddling around the halls. "He woke up with a bad cough, must have been croup. He got better in the car on the way over." Ah, cool air. Good medicine. Quiet night. An elderly man comes in with back pain. He'll be fine. Quite night.

Then, the nurse shouts out, Come quick, come quick. The man is in his 20's. He is built strong. His eyes are wide, wide open. Terror. A nightmare. His skin is blue. The color of the ocean. He takes big gasping breaths. But I do not hear breathe sounds in his lungs.

His skin is blue, the color of ice. Eyes wide. Chest heaving. Terror. Pulse thready. Unable to get a blood pressure. I look at him, at those wide eyes. Asthma? He nods yes.

As a last ditch effort before intubation, we give him a shot of adrenaline. IV goes in. A hit of steroids. Slap a nebulizer treatment on. And that's when Christmas happened for me. I look at him. He looks a little better. I say, "Hi, my name is Doctor Doolittle."

That's when Christmas happened to me. Before my eyes, his skin turns from icy gray to a light summer's day. From the blue of summer to the pink of a rose. He looks at me. He looks at my name tag, and then he smiles. He smiles that smile that says, "Is your name really Doctor Doolittle."

Sometimes all it takes is a shot of adrenaline. In the course of an hour, he went from being nearly dead to being very much alive. "Is your name really Doctor Doolittle?" he asked. Sometimes, all you need is a shot of adrenaline.

Christmas is about life, about new life. Christmas does not come with more. Christmas comes with less. These days, the newspapers are filled with pounds of inserts. On TV, we are pounded with advertisements about all the stuff we do not need. It is the slogans that I find so distasteful. For Target stores, "Get more. Pay less." For a wireless company, Catherine Zeta Jones coos, "Get more." From Sears alone, I have seen commercials for everything from power drills to diamonds. I do not know whether to laugh or to cry. Christmas is about life, about new life. Christmas does not come with more. Christmas comes with less.

This is what I mean. This is the second thought. I want to share with you a poem by my favorite poet Rainer Marie Rilke. He won the Nobel Prize in the early part of the 20th century. He is a pilgrim and a poet: two good things to be. He writes this:

> "If only for once it were still.
> If only the *not quite right* or the *why this*
> Could be muted, and the neighbor's laughter,
> And the static my senses make-
> If all of it didn't keep me from coming awake-
>
> Then in one vast thousand fold thought
> I could think you up to where thinking ends.
>
> I could possess you,
> Even for the brevity of a smile,
> To offer you,
> To all that lives,
> In gladness."*

---

* Rilke, Rainer Maria. *Rilke's Book of Hours: Love Poems to God.* Penguin, 2005, I, 7.

If I could turn down the noise, make the clutter of my mind go away. If I could tone down the expectations, the "not quite right" and the "why this" of my life. If I could open my eyes, not to more stuff, but to life....

Here we are, a world gasping for life. Here we are, heaving our chest for a true breath of fresh air. Here we are, icy, blue, and so cold. Eyes wide. Terror. There are rumors of war. We worry how much stuff we have to buy. When will my Messiah come? When will my breath come? When will my new life be borne within me? I need some adrenaline here, stat!

From the ice, the rainy night, from the darkness of the soul, a child is borne, a Son is given. He shall be called Wonderful Counselor. Emmanuel. God with Us. The wolf shall lie down with lamb, and a child shall lead them.

The people of God came to John the Baptist. He lived in the desert. He looked like a prophet. He spoke like a prophet. "Repent! Repent!" He was wild in his camel's hair cloak. The people of God came to him and asked, "Are you the Messiah?" Are you the Anointed One who will re-lease the captives and set Israel free? Are you Jesus, the One who saves?

John cries out, "I am not him. I am the voice crying out in the wilderness, 'Make straight the paths of the Lord.'" I am not the Messiah. I am the one who points to the Messiah. I am the one who proclaims that Jesus is coming. Christmas is coming.

On a cold night, in manger, wrapped in swaddling clothe, a child is borne who will save the world and will save your life. Jesus. Adrenaline. The Word made flesh. Love come down. Emmanuel. God-with-Us. In the eyes of our neighbor, look for Jesus, because he is there. In the silent night, holy night of our thoughts, pause for Jesus, because Jesus is there. In our hopes and our prayers, wait for him, because Jesus is there. He will save you. This is the Good News. Amen.

A Fool for Joy

Friends, faculty, fellow physicians, thank you so much for this happy honor to join your graduation festivities.* I am humbled: there are many famous people at Yale that you could have asked. There are wiser people, smarter people, classier people. Let my voice join their voices. Congratulations class of 2012! Well done!

Why ask me? I am a residency program director of a smallish, funky residency program. Why me? My chief qualification is that I am one of the biggest groupies of all the cool stuff that goes down at the medical school. I am the first to sign up when the email goes out for Power Day. I have read "When the Spirit Catches You" at least 100 times. I have a whole shelf at home dedicated to Dean Angoff's reading list. I am part of the Jack Hughes possee for Professional Responsibility. And I am steeped in the August Fortonian ways of NURS moments and breaking bad news. I love all that good stuff, and believe that it is so important to make a good person into a good doctor.

A little intimidated at what to say, as a good academic, I reviewed the literature. I went to YouTube and typed in "Best Commencement Speeches Ever." I got a lot of great stuff. Steve Jobs at Stanford in 2005 - 14 million hits. Conan O'Brien at Dartmouth in 2011. Oprah at Stanford in 2008. Bono at Penn in 2004. The high school valedictorian from New Jersey who delivered his entire address as a rap song. And now, 2012, Ben Doolittle at Yale. A humbling thought.

---

* Speech given to graduates of Yale Medical School on the day prior to commencement ceremony, May 17th, 2012.

242

I want to share three stories. One from West Haven. The second, a haven from the fire. And a third from Fair Haven

WEST HAVEN

It is December of my intern year. In those days, a work week was 800 hours long, snow drifts up to your neck, etc. etc. It wasn't that bad, but it was pretty rough. I was feeling down. It was dark and cold when I went into the hospital. It was dark and cold when I came home.

One day, I am post call from the wards at the VA. That morning, I get a page to a strange number - 203-709-7861. I return the page. It is Dr. Jeffrey Stein a faculty member, the clinic director, my advisor. He says, "Tonight is medicine in the arts. There will be singing and poetry and food. Everyone will be there. It will do you good.... I think you should go."

My response, garbled, encephalopathic, something about "Post call, not sure where it is, too sleepy."

He says, "I am faxing you the directions to the nurses station as we speak."

Hours later, I am leaving the hospital. I am feeling sorry for myself. It is dark and cold. I reach into my white coat. Scrunched between the reflex hammer and an ABG kit are the directions to the faculty member's home, medicine and the arts. I remember standing there in dark parking lot wondering what I should do. I could just make it.

More than that, I was in the middle of having a serious crush on a really classy beautiful lady that some friends had set me up with. I thought, "Maybe I could call Christine to see if she would go with me." It would be like the 3rd date.

I did call. She said yes. Two months later, she said yes again. We are standing on a beach in the Virgin Islands, saying vows, getting married. Yes, you heard that right. My intern year, I got married my intern year to someone I had known for just over 3 months.

I realize this might be too much information. You all are graduating anyway. Only Toks has to put up with me for another four years. There are two really important points. Jeffrey Stein, one of my teachers, cared enough to reach out to a beleaguered intern. He cared. A thoughtful, simple gesture that had a huge impact - among many of his thoughtful gestures during residency. He was the great listener, the encourager, and the model of what I hoped to be when I became an attending.

The second piece is risk. I was a fool for love, and before the voice of reason quashed the dream, before the post-call encephalopathy drove me to bed, I made a phone call that changed my life. You can't connect the dotes going forward. You can only look back and see how all the pieces fit.

In the next year, a lot of amazing things will happen to you. You are brilliant, but your intellect will be challenged. You are caring, but even Mother Theresa would get cranky at 2am for a Tylenol order. Our craft, our call, is hard. The sheer grind of suffering and human need can calcify our souls so quickly.

Despite it all, or because of it all, we are so powerfully influenced, rescued even, by the caring of others. And so, when in doubt, be a fool for love. This can be a small thing: we all know that kind intern who took the time to teach us something on a busy call night. In six weeks, you get to be that intern.

Being a fool for love can also be a big thing: What is your big idea? What is your passion? Find a job that doesn't feel like a job. I think that if you love what you do, a balanced life is overrated. In medicine, we tend to be persevering, delayed gratification types. And so, sometime during residency, take a risk. Heart on your sleeve. The embarrassing humiliation, years later becomes the stuff of family lore and comedy years. Better to risk and lose than to live in regret. We all get over it. And so, be a fool for love, in small ways, and in big.

A HAVEN FROM THE FIRE

A true story - August 4th, 1949. On that day, outside of Helena, Montana, on Merriwether Ridge, just above the Missouri River, a ranger spots a fire amidst the Douglas Fir and Ponderosa Pines. He sends out a call. The next day, a C-47 transport plane flies out of Missoula. Fifteen smokejumpers parachute onto the south ridge of Mann Gulch. They are joined by a fireguard from the US Forest service.

Standing on that ridge, the firefighters realize that the parachute containing their radio did not open. The radio crashed to the ground and is lost. But no matter. These guys are tough, seasoned, well-trained fire fighters. Wagner Dodge, their foreman, thinks it looks like a "10 o'clock fire" - meaning that by 10 am on the next day, they will have extinguished the fire.

He was wrong.

The team lands high up on the south side of ridge. Wag realizes that they need to cross over to the north side of the ridge so that the river can be at their back. With the river at their back, they would have a safe area behind them and also a way to escape.

The crew winds their way through the gulch. It is slow going because the pitch is about 75 degrees and the grass is waist high. It had been a very dry summer. Because of the bend in the land, they cannot see too well ahead. When they turn the ridge, Wag Dodge realizes that they are in trouble. The fire has crossed the river and exploded. The wall of flames is heading right towards them. Their way to the river is blocked. They have no radio. Wag Dodge orders his men back up the hill.

It is going to be close. Each man is carrying about 100 lbs of gear. They are trained never to drop their gear. If they can get to the top of the ridge they will be safe.

The grass is waist high. The ridge is steep.

The fire superheats the air. The flames gather momentum. Later, officials estimated that the fire started at 1.5 miles per hour. 10 minutes later, the firewall is travelling seven miles per hour. A wall of flame, as tall as the pillars of Sterling Hall of Medicine, blasts towards the firefighters. The air is superheated. It is getting hard to breath. Wag Dodge realizes that they are all going to die.

At the moment, when all is lost, Wag Dodge has an idea. Instead of running from the fire. He stops. He sets aflame an area of grass just ahead of him.

This escape fire burns up the hill and forms a small ellipse in front of him. He steps into the burned out circle, and lays down. He orders his men to do the same. They do not hear him. They think he is crazy or they are too terrified to think. They struggle past him, with their pick axes and heavy packs. The firewall blows past Wag Dodge, but he is unharmed. His "escape fire" has saved him.

15 men jumped out of the airplane that day and a 16th - a forest ranger - joined them. 13 of those men were burned to death in the fire. Two make it to the ridge and survive. They find a small crevice that connects to the other side of the ridge – a lucky break. The third is Wag Dodge, who

survives in his fire of safety. The 10am fire claimed the lives of 13 men in about an hour and a half.

This story comes from a book "Young Men and Fire" by Norman Maclean, but I first came across this story from Don Berwick one of the great quality innovators for healthcare. The Mann Gulch fire is a metaphor for health care. Over the years, I keep coming back to this story, because I wonder, am I Wag Dodge the foreman? Or, am I the guy dragging 100 pounds a gear being overtaken by the flames'? Are you Wag Dodge the foreman, or are you being caught in the fire? Would I have had the insight, the wisdom, the cool head amidst the chaos to come up with the escape fire? Or, would I have been a casualty? The message of the Mann Gulch fire is chilling: innovate or die.

And so, while you are on the wards, being fools for love, be also the cool head amidst the chaos. Light the escape fire. Innovate. Lead by example. Be a fool for love. Light the fire.

FAIR HAVEN

As you may know, for more than 20 years, all through medical school, residency, and to this day, I have served as an ordained minister. Over the years, I have had the great joy of officiating the weddings of many of those who have gone before you. I am forever grateful that Yale is the sort of place that encourages this sort of untraditional thing.

I am a last-ditch minister. I am the minister that a church is stuck with when there are no other choices. My first two churches had no money, were on the brink of closing, with no prospects for a replacement, in some pretty rough parts of town. What kind of church would have a medical student as their minister? Surely not a church with two dimes to scrape together to hire someone else. What kind of church would have a Yale resident as their minister? What kind of resident would be crazy enough to endeavor such as task? My first two churches - where I was the solo pastor - struggled to keep oil in the boiler every month of every year. But, both churches were rich in faith - a dogged, stubborn, unyielding, crazy faith, filled with joy, a community of hope on the ragged edge of hope in the inner city. I serve as an associate minister at a slightly larger church now.

The churches that accepted me into their fold did more than that. They loved me, as I in turn loved them. I owe a lot to the churches that took a chance on me for they have taught me a lot about perseverance and hope.

During residency, I served at the East Pearl Street Methodist Church in the Fair Haven neighborhood - a few blocks down Grand Avenue from the Fair Haven clinic. One of the first challenges that plagued our ministry was that, across the street, in a vacant lot, people were dealing drugs. It was an ideal place to sell drugs, a one-way side street, in a dark lot, filled with shadows, across from an old church that was mostly vacant at night.

As we began to have more evening meetings, and Bible studies and such, the problem became apparent. Cars lingered on the street corners, throttling their engine. We found needles on the sidewalk. We called the police. Arrests were made. But the dealers always drifted back. When we would leave the church, there was often a white Chevie with dark tinted windows that would slowly pull away from the curb when we exited the church.

Once, I noticed that the white Chevie with dark tinted windows did not drive away when we left one of our church meetings. I thought it strange, but did not give it much thought at the time. Later, I learned that the driver of that car had died of a drug overdose, in his car... across the street ... from our church.

Something had to be done. But what can you do? Church folks felt unsafe. The police knew what was going on, but the problem was everywhere. What could they do? Our neighbors were beleaguered. Everyone was frustrated. What can you do? A huge social problem had literally parked itself on our curb and stank.

This is what we did, mostly out of desperation. I channeled Nancy Reagan. When the Ronald Reagan, the Great Orator, was president, his wife launched a "Just Say No" campaign. It was really cheesy. And so, I made various signs that I would nail to the Maple tree across the street that sheltered the empty lot. "Please do not deal drugs here." "God is love. Don't do drugs." "Drug dealers please go away." It was campy. It was hokey. It was pathetic. But what else was there to say?

Every Sunday, I staple the sign to the old maple tree. The next day, the sign is gone. I staple the sign up again. A few days later, the sign is gone. This goes on for a couple of weeks.

A parishioner named Bob Dean has another idea. In the church's large stained glass window, directly across from the vacant lot, he hangs the word, "JOY" in big letters four feet high. He backlights the sign with a big spot light and puts it on a timer. When the sun goes down, the spot light beams the word JOY in big letters into the dark shadows of the vacant lot.

Now, if you dealt drugs on East Pearl Street, you did so literally in the shadow of joy. Joy. Joy. Joy. Suddenly, dealing drugs on East Pearl Street became unpleasant, distressing.

One Sunday, when I parked my car beneath the Maple tree, the sign I had hung a few days before – "God is love. Don't do drugs" – was still hanging on the tree. No one had torn it down. Wet with rain. Crinkled a bit from the weather. But there it was, still on the tree. God is love. Don't do drugs. No one had torn down the sign. The drug dealing had moved on.

We made no pretense about what we had accomplished. We did not solve the drug problem in New Haven. We did not save the man who died in that white Chevie. We did not even solve the demon of addiction that afflicted many within our own congregation. We understood that the problem was complicated, very complicated.

But we did accomplish something. You could come to this place in the evening and feel safe. You could stand in the light of joy and feel safe. The very act of going to church in the evening became a powerful witness to a new life, a new way in the neighborhood. "The light shines in the darkness and the darkness does not overcome it."

Class of 2012. Doctors. Colleagues. Friends. Be a fool for love. Be the fire of change. Be the light in the darkness. I wish you all the very best. Have a great graduation weekend. Congratulations on all that you have accomplished.

About the Author

"Brother" Ben (people really call him that) grew up outside of Schenectady NY in the foothills of the Adirondack Mountains. He got into Yale College off the waiting list and ended up staying for the nearly 30 years or so and going strong. He did a combined MD-MDIV degree at Yale, served as a medical missionary to India and Honduras after graduation, and completed a combined internal medicine-pediatrics residency. He joined the faculty in 2002 where he directs the Internal Medicine-Pediatrics residency program and serves as medical director of the faculty-resident clinic. He continues to serve the local church in a variety of capacities – supervised ministry mentor, pastor, and preacher. Ben is married to Christine and together they raise their two daughters with lots of help from Grandparents. They live in Kensington, CT.

Made in the USA
Middletown, DE
26 September 2017